THE INVASION
OF CANADA

BATTLES OF THE WAR OF 1812

Ronald J. Dale

JAMES LORIMER & COMPANY LTD., PUBLISHERS

TORONTO

James Lorimer & Company Ltd., Publishers acknowledges the support of the Ontario Arts Council. We acknowledge the financial support of the Government of Canada through the Canada Book Fund for our publishing activities. We acknowledge the support of the Canada Council for the Arts which last year invested $24.3 million in writing and publishing throughout Canada. We acknowledge the Government of Ontario through the Ontario Media Development Corporation's Ontario Book Initiative.

Cartography by Peggy McCalla

Library and Archives Canada Cataloguing in Publication

Dale, Ronald J., 1951-
The invasion of Canada : battles of the War of 1812 / Ronald J. Dale. -- New ed.

Includes bibliographical references and index.
ISBN 978-1-55277-784-8

1. Canada--History--War of 1812--Campaigns. I. Title.

FC442.D34 2011   971.03'4   C2011-900861-0

James Lorimer & Company Ltd., Publishers
317 Adelaide Street West, Suite #1002
Toronto, ON M5V 1P9
www.lorimer.ca

Distributed in the United States by:
Casemate Publishers and Book Distributors, L.L.C.
908 Darby Road
Havertown, PA 19083 USA

Printed and bound in Canada

Photo Credits

Except for the following images, all photographs in this book were taken by Dwayne Coon.

T = top; B = bottom; L = left; R = right

Anne S.K. Brown Military Collection, Brown University Library: 27; Archives of Ontario: 50T; Army Art Collection, U.S. Army Center of Military History: 73; Detroit Public Library, Burton Historical Collection: 18B; Formac Publishing: 11L, 62, 67, 68; Fort York: 43; Government of Ontario Art Collection: 18T, 33T (with permission from the estate of CW Jefferys); Historical Services Division, U.S. Department of Defense: 38; James Lorimer & Co.: 55, 55 inset (Steven Mecredy); Metro Toronto Library: 16T, 19T, 23T, 42, 56; National Archives of Canada: 41, 48, 71, 79T; Niagara Historic Society Museum: 30B, 31T; Nova Scotia Archives/Records Management: 65; Parks Canada: 10, 12, 13T, 14, 15T, 15B, 16B, 19B, 20T, 20B, 21T, 21B, 23B, 25, 26, 28B, 31B, 32, 34T, 34B, 35, 36L, 36R, 44T, 45T, 46, 49B, 53, 54, 60, 61B, 72, 79B; Peter Rindlisbacher: 17, 24, 40, 52, 59, 66; Royal Military College, Kingston: 61T; St. Lawrence Parks Commission: 57, 58; U.S. Naval Academy Museum: 63; Windsor's Community Museum: 22.

Contents

Acknowledgements

My grandfather fought in the trenches of World War I and my father was overseas as a volunteer in the Canadian Army throughout World War II. Two of my uncles fought in Europe and another in Burma during that war. My interest in the military came naturally. My mother instilled in me a love of history. Burned into my memory is the day that our regular family Sunday drive took us to Crysler's Farm and the newly opened visitor centre at the battlefield. I was deeply influenced by the exhibit and the knowledge that I was standing on the spot where the dramatic events of November 11, 1813,

unfolded. From that moment, I was intrigued by the War of 1812 and have made it a lifelong study. During my long career with Parks Canada, working to help preserve National Historic Sites and to tell their story, I have encountered many wonderful people who have eagerly shared their knowledge with me. I would like to thank my colleagues in Parks Canada and friends from other historic sites who have contributed to my understanding of our past. I would also like to thank my wife, Nancy, and my kids who have had to put up with me, sitting in our living room, notes and documents spread around my chair, as I worked on this manuscript.

BATTLES OF 1812–14

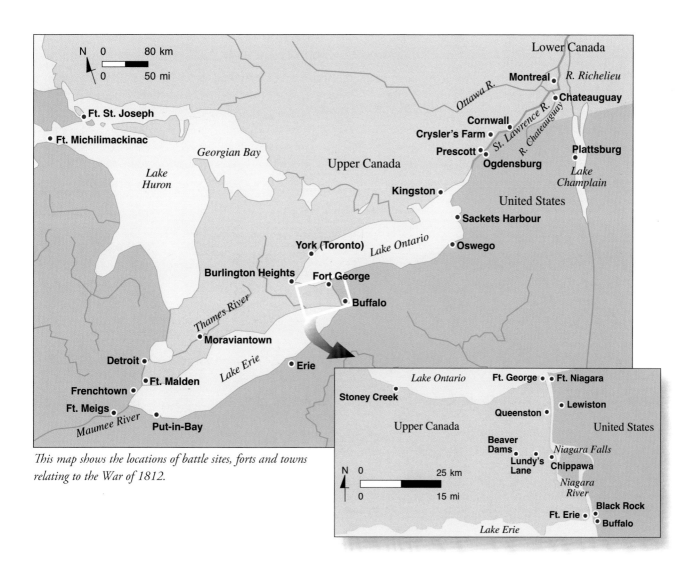

This map shows the locations of battle sites, forts and towns relating to the War of 1812.

Introduction

Throughout the 19th century, when people in the eastern half of Canada spoke of "the war," they were referring to the War of 1812. This was a North American conflict that had played a major role in the development of a Canadian identity. During the War of 1812, Canadians rallied to the call to defend their homes against the threat of invasion and annexation by the United States of America, the new republic that had ten times the population of the British colonies which later became united as Canada. During each of the three years of war, a small force of British regular army soldiers, Canadian militiamen, and Native warriors fended off American armies bent on conquest. At the same time, Royal Navy ships and Canadian "privateers" waged war on the high seas against the American maritime forces.

The War of 1812 and Canadian Identity

The War of 1812 spawned many Canadian heroes and heroines. The generations that followed were brought up with tales of General Brock's death at the Battle of Queenston Heights, Laura Secord's walk to warn the British at Beaver Dams, Tecumseh's brave stand at the Battle of Moraviantown, Charles de Salaberry's stunning victory at the Battle of Chateauguay, and the stand of the thin red line at Crysler's Farm. In Atlantic Canada, fireside tales and songs about fierce battles between brave privateersmen and "Yankee" raiders gave listeners visions of flapping sails and roaring cannons. To the present day, along the St. Lawrence, Niagara, and

(Above) The Laura Secord homestead, now a museum in Queenston. (Inset) The house's interior.

Officers' quarters at Fort George.

Detroit Rivers, families carefully preserve swords, muskets, and other relics of the war.

Some of the battlefields of the War of 1812 became early tourist attractions. Crysler's Farm, Stoney Creek, and Fort George were toured by history buffs. Generations of Canadians climbed the imposing Brock's Monument at Queenston Heights. Lundy's Lane in Niagara Falls was second only to the falls themselves as a "must-see." Until very late in the 19th century, visitors could be lectured on the battle fought here by aged veterans of the conflict, the last one being a man in his nineties who had been a young American volunteer in the battle.

More than 150 years after the end of the War of 1812, Ontario schoolchildren still sang the unofficial Canadian anthem, "The Maple Leaf Forever." The second verse is a testament to the reverence which Ontarians felt for the deeds performed by their ancestors during the war:

Bayonet belt plate from the Lincoln Militia.

> *At Queenston Heights and Lundy's Lane*
> *Our brave fathers, side by side,*
> *For freedom, homes, and loved ones dear*

> *Firmly stood and nobly died;*
> *And those dear rights which they maintained*
> *We swear to yield them never!*
> *Our watchword ever more shall be*
> *The Maple Leaf forever!*

In Eastern Canada the War of 1812 remained one of the proud eras in the new country's history until overshadowed by the bloodbaths of the 20th century's world wars. The battles of Vimy Ridge, Beaumont Hamel, Passchendaele, Ortona, and Normandy, now loom larger in the Canadian psyche, but the older fields of honour are not completely forgotten.

Preserving Our Past

By the beginning of the 20th century, many of the sacred sites of the War of 1812 were threatened by urbanization and industrial expansion. While many of the battlefields remained as farmers' fields, some of the forts had been abandoned. Fort Malden, where Brock met Tecumseh, became a mental health facility in 1851 and was later subdivided into smaller residential building lots. In the early 20th century, Lundy's Lane,

The sallyport at Ft. Mississauga. (Inset) Aerial view of Fort Mississauga.

A musket demonstration at Fort George. The fort served as the British headquarters until it was captured by the Americans in 1813.

the scene of the bloodiest battle of the war, was being swallowed by the rapidly growing city of Niagara Falls. Fort George and Fort Erie, once captured by American armies, were abandoned ruins. In Toronto, Fort York was threatened with urban and industrial expansion and came close to being destroyed for railroad development.

Some citizens recognized the need for preserving these special places and the stories which they represented. Historical societies, formed in the 1880s and 1890s, published accounts of the battles and raised funds for monuments. Canadian historians wrote popular accounts of the events, and the move for preservation grew. Brock's Monument, really the general's tomb, had been built in the 1850s to replace the earlier 1824 monument, which had been damaged in an act of terrorism in 1840. Monuments were erected to commemorate Stoney Creek, Lundy's Lane, and other heritage places. Laura Secord's bravery was recognized with a monument built on Queenston Heights by the Canadian government.

When plans were made in 1917 to demolish Toronto's Fort York to allow for the expansion of the rail lines going into the city, heritage groups were stirred to action. While Canadian minds were preoccupied with the horrors of trench warfare during World War I in Europe, an increasing sense of national pride gave Canadians an appreciation for the need to preserve the older, local battlefields and special places. Petitions and lobbying encouraged the Canadian government to establish the Historic Sites and Monuments Board of Canada (HSMB) to designate people, locations, and events of national significance, with a view of preserving those places considered to be of importance to all Canadians.

When the HSMB was formed, a number of the historic sites were already owned by the government. Some, like Fort George and Butler's Barracks in Niagara-on-the-Lake, and

Main entrance of the Halifax Citadel.

Drummond Hill Cemetery, site of the Battle of Lundy's Lane.

the Halifax Citadel in Nova Scotia, were still actively used by the military. Others were surplus to the needs of the military, which was preparing to sell the land off when the HSMB was formed. These places, beginning with Fort Anne in Annapolis Royal, Nova Scotia, were transferred to the federal Department of the Interior as National Historic Parks.

While this timely intervention saved many of the battlefields of the War of 1812, some important sites had already been lost, like Beaver Dams and Lundy's Lane. Work is currently underway to reacquire these lands for preservation. Some, like Crysler's Farm, inundated by the creation of the St. Lawrence Seaway, are lost forever. The battlefield of Chippawa was recently saved from residential development when acquired by the Niagara Parks Commission. Others, however, like the site of the Battle of Butler's Farm, are being buried under residential subdivisions. Recent house construction in the town of Fort Erie disturbed the unmarked graves of American soldiers, lying under the soil since 1814.

Although the battle for preservation continues, there are dozens of places in Canada where visitors can gain an appreciation of the stirring events of the War of 1812. Visitors can stand with the Voltigeurs Canadiens at Chateauguay, charge up Queenston Heights with General Brock, or hear the voice of Tecumseh at Moraviantown. One can also visit the carefully preserved ruins of Fort St. Joseph near Sault Ste. Marie, Ontario, or the privateers' warehouses in Halifax and Liverpool, Nova Scotia. This book is intended to help readers to understand a few of these special places where Canadians from diverse backgrounds — European, African, and Native — "firmly stood and nobly died."

1

Prelude to War: Aftermath of the American Revolution

On September 3, 1783, the Treaty of Paris was signed by Britain and representatives of the American Continental Congress, formally ending the American War of Independence and establishing the United States of America as a sovereign nation. The war had begun as an armed uprising in 1775 and had turned into a full-blown conflict resulting in a great deal of property damage and many deaths of combatants and civilians. The American Revolution had been a civil war, with the population split between those desiring independence from Britain and those wishing to continue to live under the British Constitution. When it ended, over 50,000 Americans chose to move out of the new republic and return to the British Isles or take up residence in British North America, in present-day Canada. Included among these refugees were North Americans of all colours, creeds, and nationalities, including hundreds of Six Nations people whose homes had been destroyed in the conflict.

British North America

At the time, Atlantic Canada consisted of small settlements surrounding military and naval bases, scattered and isolated farms and hamlets of Acadians who had evaded the expulsion of their people 30 years earlier, and villages of Native people located along the coasts and rivers of the colonies. Almost overnight, the arrival of Loyalist refugees during and following the American Revolution dramatically increased the population. Villages grew into towns as merchants and

The Battle of Fallen Timbers, *as painted by H.C. McBarron, showing American troops.*

Quebec 1812, *by H.T. Davies. Although Upper Canada was still sparsely populated, cities like Montreal and Quebec were becoming significant centres for trade.*

manufacturers, ship builders and mariners, fishermen and farmers, took up their new lands. By the eve of the War of 1812, the population of Atlantic Canada had grown to over 60,000.

In 1783, Quebec had an established population of French Canadians in towns and farms along the St. Lawrence River and its tributaries. Since the British conquest in 1760, many merchants, fur traders, and other businessmen had moved into the towns in Quebec, the population becoming concentrated in Montreal, Quebec City, Sorel, and Trois Rivieres. West of the Ottawa River, in the territory that would become Ontario, the land was sparsely settled by bands of Native peoples. Primarily Anishinabe or Ojibwa, they lived in small groups and ranged the forests, rivers, and shores of the Great Lakes, hunting and fishing and trading furs to the agents of the fur trade empires of the Hudson's Bay or Northwest companies.

After the fall of Ft. George, the British headquarters moved to Burlington Heights, where Dundurn Castle sits today.

The arrival of over 30,000 Loyalists in 1784 transformed this territory. Towns sprang up along the St. Lawrence River and near the key military posts of Kingston and Niagara, as well as along the Detroit River. Two large contingents of Six Nations refugees were given land near Kingston at Deseronto and along the Grand River in Ontario. The people of these settlements would become crucial to the survival of the province in 1812.

In 1791, Quebec was divided into two provinces: Lower Canada (now Quebec) and Upper Canada (now Ontario). Attracted by the bountiful and inexpensive farming land available, particularly in Upper Canada, immigrants continued to arrive in the provinces. Many came from Europe but most came from the United States. When the War of 1812 broke out, the population of Upper Canada was over 60,000 while Lower Canada had over 250,000 inhabitants.

The United States of America

The fledgling United States of America was a country that could pride itself on having fought for its independence from the most powerful nation on earth. This gave its citizens a feeling of incredible confidence in what Americans could do

View of Fort Niagara, 1804. *An important commercial route, the Niagara River would be the focus of some of the heaviest action during the War of 1812.*

when they set their collective mind to it. Laws, taxes, and policies were no longer dictated by far-off London. Americans could now make their own decisions about commerce, trade, land use, and foreign relations.

The United States had a population of over seven million people, concentrated in a number of larger cities along the Atlantic seaboard. This part of the population was largely maritime, with strongly developed mercantile interests, fishing, shipbuilding, and maritime trade carried by fleets of merchant and fishing vessels. Fortunes were made by carrying raw goods to Europe and returning with manufactured items to sell in the United States.

Inland, the number of American farmers had outgrown the amount of available land east of the Allegheny Mountains. Fur traders, trappers, and soldiers who had fought in the Ohio Valley during the Revolution had seen the richness of the lands west of the mountains and spread word of these vast tracts. The Treaty of Paris had ended

British restrictions, which tended to preserve these lands for Native inhabitants, and now waves of settlers moved west to claim the area. The Ohio and Mississippi valleys, Kentucky, and the western parts of New York and Pennsylvania became flooded with adventurers set on carving homesteads out of the wilderness. To do so, they would dispossess the Native people who lived there.

The World at War

During the period of widespread colonial expansion by the major powers in the latter half of the 18th century, wars were frequent. Colonies in India, Africa, and the West Indies were rocked by rebellion and wars of conquest. England and France had been enemies throughout the centuries, and it was a French army and navy that had proved instrumental during the American War of Independence, resulting in a British defeat at the critical Battle of Yorktown. Without the strong support of France, the United States of America would never have come into existence.

Following the French Revolution, France undertook to spread its republican ideals to the rest of the world. Under the eventual leadership of Napoleon Bonaparte, the conflict surrounding French imperialist designs became global, with Britain as the major opposition to Napoleon's attempts to expand French influence throughout the world. War between Britain and France began again in 1793 and continued into the 19th century, with a brief period of peace

A painting of a Napoleonic war charge. Because of its war with France in Europe, England did not have large numbers of troops to spare for the defence of Canada.

between 1801 and 1803. In 1805, Nelson's victory at the Battle of Trafalgar prevented an invasion of Britain by a larger French army. Britain's war with France was at its height when America declared war against Britain in 1812 and it continued throughout the War of 1812.

Free Trade and Sailors' Rights

While Napoleon's armies were able to sweep across the continent of Europe, Britain's strategy was to use its navy to blockade European ports and shut down Napoleon's supply system. From the Baltic to the Mediterranean, British ships cruised near French-controlled ports, preventing ships from leaving port and stopping the ships of neutral nations in order to keep supplies from reaching the French. Among these neutral ships were many from the new United States. British boarding parties stopped ships at sea, sometimes after firing cannon at them to make them haul-to, boarded the ships, and searched them for contraband.

Corps of Provincial Artificers, *by Garth Dittrick.*

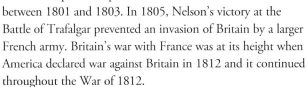

Any sailors on board the American ships were scrutinized by British officers, and those who were suspected of being deserters from the Royal Navy were seized and brought back on board British vessels. Many of these sailors had certificates "proving" American citizenship, but this did not deter the Royal Navy officers, who were perpetually short of men on their own ships. The Americans were outraged by this flagrant disregard for the sovereignty of their country.

Napoleon countered the British blockade by passing the Berlin Decree in 1806. This law dictated that any British goods carried to French-controlled ports in Europe would be seized as contraband. This would cripple British manufacturers and exporters. The British retaliated by passing Orders in Council that required every ship bound for a European port to stop first at a British port for inspection. Napoleon then issued the Milan Decree, which dictated that any ship obeying the British Orders in Council would lose its neutral status and be regarded by the French as an enemy vessel.

The disregard for the rights of neutral nations by both the British and French came close to provoking a declaration of war by the United States against Britain in 1807. This was following the "*Chesapeake* Incident," when a British warship stopped the American navy ship *Chesapeake* to search it for

Royal Navy deserters. In stopping the *Chesapeake*, the British *Leopard* opened fire on the American ship. Three American sailors were killed and 18 were wounded in the attack. Although war was narrowly avoided, the incident remained a source of American irritation.

The United States reacted to the French decrees and British Orders in Council by passing the Embargo Act, which prevented any American ships from entering foreign ports and prevented any foreign ships from carrying American goods. It was felt that the British and French would withdraw their restrictive embargo laws if the Americans cut off the shipment of American goods to Europe. This did cause shortages in Europe but also crippled the entire American mercantile industry and caused hardships among American seafarers, merchants, and manufacturers.

The violation of American neutrality, combined with the negative economic effects the United States suffered because of the Napoleonic Wars, contributed to the American declaration of war against Britain in 1812.

Tecumseh

and the rich lands of the Ohio Valley to establish homesteads, slashing and burning clearings in the forest and preventing Native hunting parties from trespassing on "their" property. Land agents and speculators acquired titles to huge tracts and resold the acreage to new settlers attracted by tales of the area's richness.

Inevitably, this unbridled expansion led to conflicts with the Native population. Many Native warriors reacted to the interlopers with violence. Skirmishes between Natives and whites became frequent, each attack inevitably leading to a retaliatory strike. At times, the government sent armies to neutralize the Native "hostiles," and treaties were negotiated to re-establish boundaries between Native territories and white settlements. These boundaries continued to be shifted westwards, however, forcing the Native people to abandon their villages and leave their ancestral lands. During this period, various Native leaders worked toward establishing Native solidarity, uniting the nations to counter the threat to their lands.

Led primarily by the Shawnee, the western tribes fought

American Westward Expansion

Following the end of the American Revolution in 1783, adventurers and frontiersmen crossed over the Allegheny Mountains to seek opportunities in the continent's vast interior. Trappers and hunters ranged over the land, competing with Native people for the increasingly scarce game. Merchants and traders, no longer as strictly regulated as they had been under a British government, travelled through Native villages. While some traders were honest, others cheated the Natives, sometimes after plying their "clients" with cheap rum. American settlers came to Kentucky

Native allies played a key role in many of the war's battles, and deserve credit for many British victories.

small parties of Americans and defeated larger American armies in 1790 and 1791. In a battle fought on November 4, 1791, the Americans sustained between 500 and 1,500 casualties. It was bloodier than most of the battles fought during the American Revolution or the War of 1812.

The victories of 1790 and 1791 showed that the Natives could be very powerful when united. The Shawnee war-chief, Tecumseh, with his brother Tenskwatawa or "the Prophet," campaigned for an alliance of all Natives to drive out the American usurpers. An American army under General "Mad Anthony" Wayne launched an expedition to squash the Native confederacy in its bud. A battle was fought at Fallen Timbers near Fort Miami on August 20, 1794, but the Natives were not defeated.

In August 1795, the Treaty of Grenville was negotiated by the American government with most of the tribes of the old Northwest territory. As a result, over the next few years thousands and thousands of acres of Native land were ceded to the land-hungry Americans.

By 1810, many of the Ohio Natives had banded together under Tecumseh and represented a genuine threat to the United States. Native warlike activity continued to increase. American general, and later president, William Henry Harrison assembled a large army to counter the Native confederacy. On November 7, 1811, while Tecumseh himself was absent far to the south of Shawnee territory, Harrison attacked Tecumseh's chief town and won a major victory in what was known as the Battle of Tippecanoe. Harrison found many British muskets and war axes on the battlefield and accused the British of arming his enemies.

Increasingly, frontier "war hawks" called for a war against the British in North America. The threat to American sovereignty on the high seas and the perceived British interference

A painting by Peter Rindlisbacher, depicting the American naval base of Sackets Harbour on Lake Ontario, as it would have appeared during the war.

in the western territories were too much for a proud young nation to bear. American rights had to be defended. Even though the British promised to withdraw the Orders in Council and their diplomats met with their counterparts in Washington to preserve the peace, this did not mollify American anger. On June 18, 1812, the United States of America declared war on the most powerful nation on earth. Canada would be the main battleground, and it was fervently hoped that an American victory would end the Native resistance, re-establish American sovereignty on the high seas, and add the rich agricultural lands of Upper Canada, the forests of Lower Canada and New Brunswick, and the fisheries of Nova Scotia and Prince Edward Island to the United States.

There was no thought of fighting a naval war with Britain. The United States Navy consisted of only 17 ocean-going vessels, the largest being the 44-gun frigates *President*, *United States*, and *Constitution*, supported by five smaller frigates, two corvettes, and eight tiny schooners, sloops, and brigs. The Royal Navy was the largest in the world, with over 800 vessels including numerous battleships that dwarfed the largest craft of the U.S. Navy.

The colonies of British North America, on the other hand, looked like easy pickings. The population of the United States was ten times larger than the populations of the Atlantic provinces and Upper and Lower Canada. Furthermore, most of the inhabitants of Upper Canada were expatriate Americans who had taken up cheap land in Upper Canada and had only been there for a few years. With Britain in a life and death struggle in Europe, Canada was lightly defended by regular soldiers. The feeling was that taking the British colonies would be, in the words of Thomas Jefferson, "a mere matter of marching."

2

The Capture of Detroit

The declaration of war by the Americans left General George Prevost, commander of the British forces in Canada, with some difficult strategic decisions. Britain was already overburdened with fighting Napoleon's forces in Europe and throughout the world and could spare few additional troops for the defence of Canada, at least in the short term. There were just over 4,300 British soldiers stationed in Newfoundland, New Brunswick, Prince Edward Island, and Nova Scotia and 5,500 in Lower Canada while Prevost's Upper Canadian commander, Major-General Isaac Brock, commanded only 1,600 men stretched over a 1,000-kilometre border with the United States. All Canadians between the ages of 16 and 60 were eligible for service in the militia but these men were untrained and poorly armed. Still, it was felt that several thousand militiamen could be called up to reinforce the regular forces. Facing the British, the Americans could field about 12,000 regulars, most of whom had been recently recruited and were therefore untrained, and as many as 80,000 militiamen.

Further, Prevost still hoped for peace and was reluctant to make any aggressive moves against the Americans. His strategy was to keep his forces concentrated at major posts in the Maritimes, Quebec, and Montreal to allow for easy reinforcement from Britain when

View of Detroit *by E.H. (Inset) Major-General Isaac Brock, by J.W.L. Forster.*

The British expected an attack to come from Sackets Harbour, the major American naval base on Lake Ontario.

troops could be spared.

While it was fully expected that the Americans would attack Upper Canada first, Prevost felt that if the province was captured by the Americans, and the British were able to retreat to Montreal and Quebec City and defend these strongpoints, eventually more troops from Britain would enable him to retake Upper Canada. The fiery, 46-year-old Isaac Brock would be left to his own devices to stall or prevent an American capture of Upper Canada.

Assembling the Forces

Brock's small army of veteran soldiers from the British Isles along with the Glengarry Light Infantry Fencibles and Canadian Fencibles, recruited in Canada and trained as regulars, were concentrated in British forts that guarded the most vulnerable points of the strategically crucial St. Lawrence River–Great Lakes transportation route. The soldiers garrisoned Kingston, Fort York (Toronto), Fort George (Niagara-on-the-Lake), Fort Erie, Fort Malden (or Amherstburg), and Fort St. Joseph on the island of that name in the mouth of the St. Mary's River, near Sault Ste. Marie. Kingston, the main Lake Ontario dockyard; Amherstburg, the location of the Lake Erie dockyard; and Fort George, the headquarters in southern Ontario, were the key posts and

the most likely targets of an American attack launched from either Sackets Harbour, Kingston's counterpart across Lake Ontario; Fort Detroit, located 30 kilometres up the Detroit River from Amherstburg; or Fort Niagara, a few hundred metres from Fort George, across the Niagara River.

While Brock could theoretically call out the militia of Upper Canada, numbering almost 11,000 men, he could arm only a portion of them. Further, because the majority of these men were relatively recent American immigrants, he was not sure if he could trust them to fight against their former countrymen. He questioned the loyalty of all but those who were British-born or whose families had been Loyalists during the Revolution. Brock requested aid from the Six Nations of Grand River, who could theoretically field 300 men.

A Private of the Glengarry Light Infantry in work dress.

Fort St. Joseph, by Edward Walsh. *As soon as war was declared, Brock ordered the troops here to attack the better-defended Ft. Michilimackinac.*

Agents of the British Indian Department at Amherstburg also remained on friendly terms with those Natives who had joined the Shawnee war chief Tecumseh to enlist their support in the coming conflict. At Fort St. Joseph in the old Northwest, the Anishinabe people were ready to ally themselves with the British against the American threat. However, Brock did not know how many Native warriors would join in the fight and was unsure of how effective they would be in a defensive war against the Americans.

Brock was a bold and decisive commander. On learning of the declaration of war, he sent a message to Captain Roberts, commander of the small garrison of Fort St. Joseph, ordering him to assemble what forces he could from the merchants and traders settled near the fort and from the Native population of the area, and to attack the American Fort Michilimackinac, a stronger garrison on the upper Great Lakes.

Roberts' garrison and the merchant militia were accompanied by canoe-loads of Natives from the Ottawa, Ojibwa, Winnebago, and other nations, including some Sioux who had travelled hundreds of miles to visit Fort St. Joseph just as the war broke out. Arriving secretly at Mackinac Island on which the American fort was located,

British Indian Department interpreter and Six Nations warrior, portrayed by staff at Fort George.

Roberts had a small cannon hauled up a hill overlooking Fort Michilimackinac. The American commander was unaware that war had been declared, as the orders from his own government had been sent by regular U.S. Mail to Cleveland, by courier to

Siege of Detroit, *by J.C.H. Forster. Although outnumbered two to one, Brock and the Canadians captured Detroit in August of 1812.*

Detroit, and forwarded from there to Michilimackinac, while Roberts had been informed directly by fast couriers dispatched by Prevost and Brock. Roberts informed the American commander, Lieutenant Porter Hanks, that war had been declared, pointed out that he had cannon trained on the American fort and that he had a much larger force of soldiers and Natives surrounding the post. Hanks surrendered the fort on July 17, 1812, without a shot being fired.

General William Hull

While Roberts was assembling his men at St. Joseph, an American army was marching to reinforce Detroit. American General William Hull, an elderly veteran of the Revolution, had set out with his army for Detroit prior to the declaration of war. As he reached the Maumee River, not far from Detroit, he hired the schooner *Cuyahoga* to carry part of his force and his baggage to Detroit. Again, the British at Fort

Malden in Amherstburg learned of the declaration of war before Hull had been informed. The British schooner *General Hunter* set out from Amherstburg and quickly captured the *Cuyahoga* before the Americans knew that their country had declared war. On board were Hull's papers, the U.S. army musicians accompanying the troops, and the wives of the officers of Hull's army. The women, along with personal baggage belonging to Hull and his men, were returned to the Americans, but the British kept Hull's papers, a

U.S. Militia Officer's Coatee from Fort Malden.

Baby House in Windsor was taken by Hull and used as his headquarters. At the time of the war, this house would have had a third storey. It is now maintained by the Windsor Community Museum.

prime source of military intelligence.

Hull experienced no further setbacks and arrived at Detroit on July 7, 1812, with 2,000 men, most of whom were recently raised militia. Another 1,500 reinforcements were to follow. The British at Amherstburg had only 300 regulars. On the American side of the river were 300 "Canadians," or men of French descent, who were considered to be of military age. Many of these men would support the British, not the American cause. Further, there were about 700 members of the militia on the Canadian side, all of the men between 16 and 60 years of age, but of course only a portion of these could be called up by the British to help in the war effort. More importantly, there were over 2,000 Native warriors from several Nations, many of whom could be expected to help Tecumseh and, therefore, the British, in the coming struggle against the Americans.

On July 12, General Hull crossed the Detroit River with an army of about 1,000 men to begin the conquest of Upper Canada. Initially, by capturing Sandwich (Windsor), directly across from Detroit, he was able to control river traffic by mounting cannons on both banks of the narrow channel. He also received orders from the Secretary of War to proceed 30 kilometres downriver to capture Fort Malden in Amherstburg.

Immediately after the invasion, Hull sent an advance guard toward Amherstburg to reconnoitre. This troop rode to the Canard River, which created an obstacle to the advance on Amherstburg, and found it guarded by two soldiers of the British 41st Regiment of Foot. They quickly overwhelmed these two sentries, killing one and mortally wounding the other, causing the first British army casualties of the war. The Americans held the bridge, and word was sent back to Hull, still in Sandwich, informing him that the way was open for an advance on Fort Malden. Hull, however, was not a hasty man. He decided that he needed heavy cannon to properly storm Fort Malden, and while he had plenty of these back at Detroit, there were no mobile "travelling" gun carriages to make their transport easy over rough terrain. He suggested that it would take two weeks to build the new carriages and withdrew the troops from the Canard River.

With second thoughts on the Canard River bridge, he sent some of his troops back on July 15, but these men found the bridge held against them by a few regular soldiers and militiamen with a small cannon. After a brief skirmish, the Americans withdrew.

British Commander-in-chief George Prevost, *by George Berthon.*

Hull dallied for the next two weeks in Sandwich, waiting for reinforcements to arrive at Detroit and for the completion of his new cannon carriages. During this time, Canadian militiamen from Essex and Kent Counties deserted in droves and in some cases turned their coats, offering to fight on the American side. They then proceeded to lead American patrols to supply caches throughout the countryside and shamelessly plundered the farms of their former neighbours. These men must have felt that the American army could not be defeated and wished to be on the winning side in the conflict.

Back at Fort George in Niagara, Brock had learned of Hull's invasion and of the desertion of many of the militia in the area. In a letter to commander-in-chief George Prevost written on July 20, Brock expressed his concern over the defeatist attitude that had developed on the Detroit frontier and of his need to keep up a brave front. "Most of the people have lost all confidence," he wrote. "I however speak loud and look big." He knew that if he left Hull's advance unchecked, or worse, if Fort Malden fell, the militia of Upper Canada and many of the Native warriors would cease to aid the British cause. Although the official British strategy was to remain on the defensive and make no moves which might provoke and increase American support for this unpopular war, Brock was a man of action.

Brock was not only the military commander in Upper Canada but was also the province's "administrator," or acting Lieutenant-Governor. On August 1, he travelled to the capi-

tal at York (Toronto) to try to convince the Upper Canadian legislature of the serious nature of the war, to persuade it to put more teeth in the militia act, to suspend *habeas corpus* during the war, and to have more money voted to aid the war effort. He found the legislature less than supportive. On August 6, after receiving a few concessions from the legislators, he dissolved parliament and set off with a contingent of York militia for Burlington Heights (Hamilton). He proceeded overland to a harbour near Port Talbot on Lake Erie, where he met with 40 regular soldiers and men of the Lincoln, Oxford, and Norfolk militia who had previously been ordered to assemble here. Brock and his small army were about to set off on an adventure that would result in the most effective bluff of the war. On August 11, Brock embarked his 40 regulars and 200 militia men into bateaux and began the long trip by water to Amherstburg.

In the meantime, things had not gone well for General Hull. He had still made no headway against Fort Malden, and remained concerned about the number of Native warriors on the flanks of his army. His supply line was precarious because the British controlled the river and Lake Erie with their small fleet of brigs and schooners based at the King's Navy Yard at Amherstburg.

The value of the control of the river was made painfully obvious on August 5, when a force of 70 British regulars under Captain Muir and 100 warriors under Tecumseh

Upper Canadian militiaman.

Bombardment of Detroit: *Queen Charlotte* and *General Hunter* off Sandwich, *by Peter Rindlisbacher.*

crossed over from Malden to the American shore and attacked a detachment of American troops and a supply train at Brownstown, almost directly opposite Amherstburg.

Hull soon learned of this setback and also learned that the Wyandots of Detroit, who had remained neutral, were now siding with the British. Fearing that he could be cut off, he retreated back across the river with his small army, returning to Detroit on August 8. His month in Sandwich had achieved very little, and his inaction combined with this retreat disconcerted his own troops while giving heart to the British and their Native allies. On August 9, an American army of 600 left Detroit to drive the small British and Native force from Brownstown. Halfway between Brownstown and Detroit, at a settlement called Maguaga, Muir with 75 regulars and 60

militia and Tecumseh with 190 men ambushed this force. The British suffered heavy casualties and were forced to retreat back to Brownstown, but the Americans had also been roughly handled and retreated back to Detroit.

Four days after the action at Maguaga, Brock's boatloads of soldiers finally reached Amherstburg just before midnight. A cheer rang through the air and soon the Native warriors camped on Bois Blanc Island began joyously firing their muskets into the air, pleased that the British seemed to finally be reinforcing Malden. Tecumseh paddled to Amherstburg to meet the British general. The two leaders spoke briefly and agreed to meet the next morning to discuss plans.

On the morning of August 14, Brock outlined his bold intention to cross the river and attack Detroit. Although he knew that the entire force available to him was outnumbered two to one by Hull and that the Americans were strongly entrenched behind the defences of Fort Detroit, he nonetheless "spoke loud" and exuded confidence. Reportedly, Tecumseh turned to some of the other principal warriors at the meeting and said of Brock, "this is a man."

That morning, Brock ordered a heavy artillery battery to be prepared at Sandwich. The following day, August 15, Brock arrived at Sandwich with his troops and ordered this battery of five guns to open fire on Detroit. The Americans returned fire, but even though the range was relatively short, little damage was caused by either side. Brock began to transport his small army across the river, and by August 16, all had disembarked. With Brock and Tecumseh were 300 regulars, 400 militia, and 600 Native warriors. Three pieces of field artillery had also been hauled along. Hull faced this force with over 2,500 men and 33 cannon, all protected behind the walls of Detroit.

It was at this point that Brock's bluff unfolded. British regulars were recognized throughout the world as the best troops anywhere. However, militia were not well trained and were inexperienced and therefore did not command the same respect as regulars. Brock had gathered the old coats of the 41st Regiment, in storage since the receipt of that year's supply of new clothing, and issued a red coat to each militiaman. What the Americans perceived was not an army of 300 regulars supported by 400 militia, but a formidable force of 700 British regulars.

Tecumseh's warriors, staying out of gunshot range of Fort Detroit, moved at the edge of the forest, in view of the American garrison. They would melt into the forest, only to appear in another clearing, giving the impression that their numbers were much higher. According to legend, Brock also orchestrated the preparation of a dispatch which was

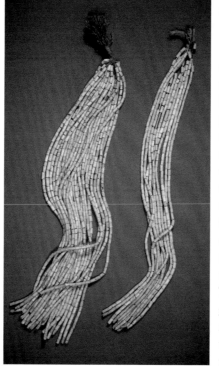

Wampum strands believed to have belonged to Tecumseh, preserved at Fort Malden.

allowed to fall into enemy hands. It was supposedly a letter to Captain Roberts at Michilimackinac, ordering him to try to prevent the large number of warriors from the upper Great Lakes from coming to Detroit to help, as Brock already had a huge army of Natives who had arrived to drive out the Americans. Prior to crossing the river from Sandwich, Brock had demanded the surrender of Detroit and, in his letter to Hull, played on Hull's fears of an "Indian massacre":

> It is far from my inclination to join in a war of extermination; but you must be aware that the numerous body of Indians who have attached themselves to my troops, will be beyond my control the moment the contest commences.

Brock paraded his troops to try to draw the Americans out of the fort to do battle on the plain. When this proved unsuccessful, he decided to assault the fort — a very hazardous and courageous undertaking.

General Hull Surrenders

Before attacking the fort, Brock sent another message to Hull demanding his capitulation, again playing on Hull's fears of a massacre. This time, Hull gave in and surrendered the fort, the town, the garrison, and the entire territory of Michigan. Brock's 1,300 men watched as 2,500 American soldiers marched by, dropping their muskets onto piles and awaiting their fate. Some of the American officers were appalled by Hull's actions and broke their swords over their knees rather than hand them over to the redcoats. There were too many Americans to guard, so Brock "paroled" 1,600 Ohio militiamen. This parole system allowed them to return to their homes if they promised not to fight again until they were exchanged with a similar number of British who had been captured. The

Surrender of Detroit, by J.C.H. Forster. By dressing militiamen in old uniforms, Brock tricked the Americans into thinking they faced a much larger force of regulars than they really did.

rest of Hull's army began a march to captivity that ended in Montreal. Hull eventually returned to the United States where he was tried and condemned to death for cowardice by a court martial. The President, however, overturned the sentence "in consideration of his age and services during the war of independence," and Hull was discharged from the army in dishonour.

The capture of Detroit swung the Native nations firmly behind the British. It also put backbone into the wavering Essex and Kent militia, and gave Brock much-needed arms and ammunition and a host of supplies for equipping the militia. This victory also resulted in the participants eventually receiving "prize money," a reward for the valuable items seized. Following the surrender, Brock took off his red silk sash, a symbol of rank worn by all officers, and presented it

to Tecumseh. Tecumseh removed his own finger woven wool sash and gave it to Brock, who would wear it for the rest of his short life. On learning of Brock's success, the British government elevated him to the Order of Bath. Although he was Sir Isaac Brock by October 1812, he would be dead before he could learn of this new honour.

With Detroit firmly in friendly hands, Brock could not tarry on that frontier. He knew that Niagara was threatened and he wanted to be in the heat of action when that front was tested. He ordered many of Detroit's cannon to be sent to Amherstburg and Fort George to make up deficiencies in the armaments of those posts and was able to distribute captured American muskets and ammunition to the militia and to his Native allies. At Niagara, Brock would soon need all of the men that he could gather.

3

THE BATTLE OF QUEENSTON HEIGHTS

Major-General Isaac Brock returned to Fort George on August 24. The previous day, upon arriving at Fort Erie from Detroit, he learned that an armistice agreement had been signed by the American commander Henry Dearborn and the British commander-in-chief, George Prevost. Prevost had learned that the British Orders in Council, one of the factors motivating the American declaration of war, had been withdrawn and he had suggested the armistice in the hope that the war could be brought to a peaceful conclusion. Although this armistice was ended by the Americans, effective September 8, 1812, Prevost was still hopeful that peace could be negotiated, provided that the British did nothing to anger the Americans. Brock was ordered to make no offensive moves and to simply remain

A painting by J.D. Kelly, depicting the Battle of Queenston Heights and the fall of Brock. Although this battle would make Brock a legend in Canada, he would not live to see its resolution.

Fort Niagara, as it is seen from the Canadian shore today. Fewer than 1,400 regulars, militia, and Native warriors defended the Canadian side of the river, while the American side boasted a force of up to 6,000.

on the defensive. Brock seemed to foresee, however, that the war would continue, and he watched helplessly through September as the American army increased its presence along the Niagara frontier while few British reinforcements were made available to him.

By late September, Brock's force of 600 regular troops of the 41st and 49th regiments, augmented by a similar number of Upper Canadian militia from Lincoln and York counties, were spread out along the Niagara River, stationed at Fort George, Queenston, Chippawa, and Fort Erie, and at several key spots between these larger posts. In the neighbourhood were about 250 Six Nations warriors under war-chiefs John Norton and John Brant, who could be counted on to help in an emergency. On the American side of the Niagara River, American militia Major-General Stephen Van Rensselaer commanded as many as 6,000 men, half of whom were regulars.

The balance was not as skewed as the numbers would indicate, however. Most of the American regulars were recent recruits, untested and untrained. Regular and militia officers, including the commanding officer, were inexperienced. The disorganized supply system meant that

John Brant, *by Ralph Tremblay.*

many went without food for long periods of time and shivered at night without tents or even blankets to drive off the autumn chill. The troops were poorly clothed and some of the American soldiers were even barefoot. Poor sanitation in the camps resulted in outbreaks of disease, which kept large numbers of men out of action. In addition, discipline among some regiments was nonexistent. To make matters worse, the regular United States Army officers objected to being under the command of Stephen Van Rensselaer, a political appointee who was a New York militia officer without much experience. When regular U.S. Army Brigadier-General Alexander Smyth (who had been a militia officer until recently) arrived on the frontier in the third week of September, many (including Smyth) thought that he should take command from Van Rensselaer, but this was not to be the case and the regular officers remained uncooperative. A mood of divisiveness pervaded the entire American force.

Brock was aware that it was only a matter of time before the Americans invaded Niagara. He noticed that they were building their army on the Niagara River frontier during September and recognized that the odds were stacking up against the British. He wanted to mount a pre-emptive attack on the Americans while they were disorganized, but his hands were tied by Prevost's insistence that he remain on the defensive as long as there was any chance of peace being negotiated. On September 18, Brock wrote to his brother: "I firmly believe that I could at this moment sweep everything before me from Fort Niagara to Buffalo." He went on to predict that within two weeks, his brother would hear of "some decided action" at Niagara whereby, if the Americans were successful, "the Province is inevitably gone." Brock also regretted that he remained stationed in North America, thus failing to gain glory fighting against Napoleon in Europe. Ultimately, his prediction of the "decided action" would come true, and although he could not join Wellington in Europe, he did, ironically, gain the glory which he sought.

Brock expected that an American invasion could be launched against any point along the Niagara River from Fort Erie to Fort George, a 50-kilometre stretch of border manned by the 1,200 men at his disposal. He had to keep a close eye on any American movements in order to anticipate when and where they would land, so that he could concentrate his forces to meet any attack. He knew that a last contingent of American militia were on their way to reinforce those already gathered on the frontier. He wrote to Prevost that "after the whole arrive, an attack, I imagine cannot be long delayed. The wretched state of their quotas [of militia] and the raggedness of their troops, will not allow them to brave the rain and cold."

Garrison gun at Fort Erie with the Niagara river in the background. This cannon could reach the American shore.

The American Invasion

Brock was right. The American troops concentrated along the Niagara River, from Fort Niagara to Buffalo, were growing increasingly restless with inaction and American sentries frequently fired across the Niagara River at British sentries. The muskets of the day were short-range weapons, and very little damage was done by those taking pot-shots at the Canadian shore. Nonetheless, this was considered ungentle-

manly behaviour and Brock sent letters of protest to Van Rensselaer to the effect that this type of action was uncivilized. Van Rensselaer agreed, but discipline in the American army was such that he was powerless to stop the sniping. Of more concern to Van Rensselaer were the desertions, which were increasing in number every day.

On October 8, two sailing ships, the British brig *Detroit* and the Northwest Company brig *Caledonia*, arrived from Detroit and anchored at Fort Erie. In the early hours of October 9, a United States Navy force, along with some regular army soldiers, rowed across from the American shore and climbed aboard the vessels, sailing them back toward the American gun batteries at Black Rock. The British shore batteries opened fire and the *Detroit* grounded on a nearby island while the *Caledonia* was brought safely to the U.S. shore. The *Detroit* was reboarded by British troops, who were forced off heights are part of the Niagara Escarpment overlooking the small village of Queenston, the farthest point upriver that ships could navigate and the beginning of the portage road that bypassed Niagara Falls. From the heights, one could see the roads on both sides of the Niagara River all the way to Lake Ontario. Ships could be spotted on Lake Ontario when they were still far out on the lake. By capturing Queenston, the Americans would be able to cut the communications route into the western portions of Upper Canada, thereby isolating the Detroit frontier. Furthermore, they could use it as a bridgehead from which to launch an attack on nearby Fort George and they would be able to watch for any British reinforcements coming by road or by water. A successful landing at Queenston would be the first stage in the conquest of the entire province.

Prior to setting his final plans for the invasion, Van Rensselaer wrote to Brigadier-General Smyth at Buffalo suggesting that they get together and make plans. Smyth never replied to this request. From that point forward, the attack was disastrous for the Americans. In the late afternoon of October 11, the American army assembled at Lewiston's ferry dock, opposite the village of Queenston. The boats to be used for the crossing were tied up elsewhere, and experienced rivermen under the command of a Lieutenant Sim were to bring the boats by water to the embarkation point. Sim drifted past this point, tied his boat to the shore, and was never seen again. Some of the other boats arrived at the right place but most of the oars had been in the lead boat commanded by Sim. The soldiers had stood at the ready for a good part of the night, waiting to invade, when the invasion was postponed while someone was sent to look for Sim's boat and the wayward oars. Soon a violent storm broke, with cold weather and driving rain lasting 28 hours and rendering the flintlock muskets of the soldiers useless. The invasion was rescheduled for October 13.

Brock had been watching American

View from Queenston Heights, where a monument to Laura Secord now stands.

by American gunfire. An American party later returned and burned the brig.

The naval action seemed to spur on the American militia, who were demanding either action or permission to retire to their homes for the winter. Van Rensselaer had been ordered to attack Canada before winter, and a piece of false intelligence to the effect that Brock had ordered most of his garrison to the Detroit frontier made the time seem ripe. On October 8, Van Rensselaer wrote to William Eustis, the Secretary of War, that "the crisis in this campaign was rapidly advancing and that the blow must soon be struck or all the toil and expense of the campaign will go for nothing." A decision had been made. Van Rensselaer planned the invasion for October 11. He would make an amphibious landing at the village of Queenston.

Queenston Heights was a very strategic location. The

Brock's hat, preserved by the Niagara Historical Society Museum.

Flintlock pistol carried by a British officer during the War of 1812, preserved by the Niagara Historical Society Museum.

movements, counting the tents that sprang up in Lewiston, observing the gathering of barges in the river, questioning American deserters and receiving reports from spies to try to determine American plans so that he could deploy his troops to the best advantage. He suspected that Van Rensselaer would launch a feint attack at Queenston to draw off the forces from Fort George and then launch a determined attack on Fort George after most of its garrison had been rushed off to Queenston. The American fiasco of October 11 seemed like a failed feint. The Americans were so careless in deploying their troops in full view of the British at Queenston, so open in their plan to embark troops at Lewiston, and were so visible while erecting new batteries of cannon on Lewiston Heights, that everything must have seemed far too obvious to ring true. Therefore, Brock kept only two companies of regulars, about 150 men, and a similar number of militiamen stationed at this vulnerable point. He kept the bulk of his forces in and around Fort George, where he thought the real landing would take place. The regular troops at Queenston, the Grenadier and Light companies of the 49th Regiment, were the best fighting men in the regiment but were also displaying signs of insubordination and even mutiny. Brock had dispatched Major Evans to deal with the disciplinary problems, and Evans was able to bring the recalcitrant men under control within 24 hours of the American invasion.

During the night of October 12

A sergeant of the Royal Artillery, painted by Charles Stadden.

and into the early morning hours of October 13, American soldiers, 300 of whom were regulars under Lieutenant-Colonel Christie and a similar number of militia under Van Rensselaer's nephew, Colonel Solomon Van Rensselaer, filed down to the Lewiston landing docks and quietly embarked into the waiting boats. At about 3:00 a.m., the first boats neared the Canadian shore and were fired on by an alert sentry at the Queenston dock. Soon the small garrison of Queenston, on the alert since the fiasco of October 11, swung into action. The Grenadier and Light companies of the 49th, the ill-disciplined, mutinous men of the previous day, reacted with professional precision, standing on the bank of the river in two ranks, loading and firing their muskets four times a minute, raining a hail of lead down on the American boats, which had to fight a 12-knot current to cross the river. Soon the militia stationed at the town entered the battle, and the large cannons at the Redan battery, halfway up the heights, and Vrooman's battery, a few hundred metres down river, joined a couple of small field guns in firing loads of lethal canister and grape-shot at the advancing enemy. American cannon on Lewiston Heights fired back at the British guns, and soon the night was filled with noise of battle, the crack of muskets, the roar of cannon, and the cries of the wounded.

The first wave of invaders, led by Colonel Solomon Van Rensselaer, hit the shore at Queenston but were pinned down by musket fire. Every officer was wounded and had to be evacuated. Van Rensselaer was hit by several musket balls, but refused to be evacuated even though he was faint from the loss of blood and shot through both legs. With the dark night illuminated only by the flash of muskets and cannon and the "fog of war" from the smoke

Aerial view of Fort George, which has been restored to its 1812 appearance.

of exploding gunpowder, more American boats were able to disembark soldiers at Queenston. A squad of soldiers under Captain Wool of the 13th Infantry climbed the heights via a narrow fisherman's path. Eventually, a fairly large American squad was stationed above the Redan battery. Charging down the heights, the Americans chased the small squad of British gunners from the Redan battery, but not before the professional Royal Artillerymen "spiked" the cannon, driving a nail into the touch-hole to make the gun inoperable and thereby prevent its use by its captors.

The Death of Brock

Eight kilometres downriver, Brock was wakened by the first rumbles of artillery fire from Queenston. Brock quickly assembled his officers and gave them his orders. He still expected that the attack on Queenston was a feint and ordered the bulk of the garrison of Fort George, under his second-in-command, Major-General Roger Hale Sheaffe, to keep alert for any signs of American movement from the other side of the river and to proceed to Queenston only if it was obvious that no other attack would be forthcoming. Brock's aides-de-camp, John Macdonell and John Glegg, were ordered to Queenston along

with the flank companies of the 41st Regiment and the men of the Lincoln and York militia.

Brock galloped along the river road to Queenston, pausing along the way to order a company of York militia to proceed to the battlefield in haste. His order, "Push on York Volunteers," became a battle cry for generations of Toronto militiamen. When Brock arrived at the beleaguered village, it was still drizzling, the sky was overcast, the pall of powder-smoke obscured everything, and musket balls buzzed overhead while cannonballs fired from Lewiston struck the stone buildings of Queenston. A loud cheer was heard from up on the heights, and the retreating crew from the Redan battery soon reported the American capture of that key position.

Brock realized the significance of the capture of the Redan battery. If the Americans could unspike the cannon there, a heavy 18-pounder gun, they could cover the landing by the remainder of their army and all would be lost. Brock gathered together a force of perhaps 100 regulars and militia, drew his sword, and led his men on a mad charge to retake the Redan. He did not get far. An American infantryman stepped forward only metres from where Brock strode, levelled his musket, and fired at the imposing figure of Brock. The American's double-shotted musket could not miss the general,

Death of Brock at Queenston Heights by C.W. Jefferys. When Brock fell, his aide-de-camp, John Macdonell, rallied the troops. They charged up the hill and, almost at the Redan, Macdonell was shot and fell. He died 20 hours later.

who at 6'3" in height, and perhaps 240 pounds, made a very large target. Brock clasped his chest and fell. His troops faltered and retreated.

Brock's provincial aide-de-camp, Canadian-born Lieutenant-Colonel John Macdonell, rallied the troops and led another charge. Riding his horse through a cloud of American musket balls, Macdonell had almost reached the Redan when his horse was hit, and when it turned and reared, Macdonell was shot in the back. He would live another 20 hours in agony before finally succumbing to this fatal wound.

Gun limbers at Fort George.

Victory at Queenston Heights

As dawn broke on the morning of October 13, the fate of Upper Canada looked bleak. Brock was dead, his body retrieved and concealed in one of the buildings in the village. The Americans held the heights and the Redan battery position, and more American troops were being ferried across the Niagara from Lewiston, joining their comrades on the heights. By late morning, they had landed 1,300 men and a six-pounder field gun, and were able to unspike the large cannon in the Redan Battery. The British and Canadian troops had retreated to the north end of the village to Vrooman's battery, where the cannon there continued to fire at the Americans.

However, help was on the way. Back at Niagara, Fort George was hotly engaged in an artillery duel with Fort Niagara, and soldiers from both sides were kept busy dousing fires caused by the shelling. At one point, Fort George was

The British position at Chippawa, *by S. Stretton. Reinforcements from Chippawa and Ft. George turned the tide of the battle.*

abandoned when its powder magazine was hit by a red-hot cannonball, but an intrepid body of volunteers was able to douse the fire before the embers could reach the gunpowder. It was obvious to General Sheaffe that the American attack at Queenston was not a feint but the main event. Acting on Brock's previous orders, he ordered all available men to hasten to Queenston, leaving a garrison at Fort George large enough to continue to fire the fort's cannon at Fort Niagara. Earlier, the British garrison of Chippawa had been ordered to march toward the sound of battle.

About 100 Six Nations warriors under John Norton, with a number of militiamen, raced on ahead of Sheaffe's marching reinforcements and arrived at Queenston to find the Americans digging in on the heights. Scaling the escarpment, these men carried out a guerilla warfare-type action which proved crucial to the day's final outcome. By occupying the woods at the summit of Queenston Heights and maintaining a steady fire on the American

John Norton, war chief of the Mohawk, *by Thomas Philips.*

lines, the Natives with their militia allies were able to keep the Americans from exploiting their position or from organizing the next phase of their invasion. The Americans were kept pinned down while Sheaffe's reinforcements arrived and were carefully deployed for the final battle.

While the number of American soldiers on Canadian soil still outnumbered all of the men available to General Sheaffe, they had many wounded in their ranks and needed reinforcements to make their victory complete. Unfortunately for them, there were over 4,000 soldiers still in Lewiston who refused to cross to Queenston to help. These untrained men clearly saw the lines of British reinforcements marching from Fort George. While there were only a few hundred of them, their red coats could be seen miles away and the frightened American militia estimated that their numbers were much higher. Further, the sight of the moaning wounded who had been evacuated from the Canadian shore and the fierce cries of the Six Nations warriors carried on the wind struck fear in many American hearts. Hundreds of militiamen from New York and Pennsylvania refused to obey orders, standing on their constitutional right to not have to fight outside of the United States. They chose to leave their comrades on the heights to their fate. The Americans, now under the command of Lieutenant-Colonel Winfield Scott, continued to prepare light field defences on top of the heights while skirmishing with the Natives and Canadian militia who hemmed them in.

Sheaffe's main body of troops had arrived at Vrooman's Point, and the new commander of

Re-enacters demonstrating battle tactics of the War of 1812.

the British forces assessed the situation carefully. American guns from Lewiston and the now operating gun of the Redan ploughed furrows through the fields near the village and ricocheted off its stone buildings but could not reach his troops. Sheaffe decided that he needed to confront the stranded American army on the heights, but wanted to get his force into position safely. He marched his men obliquely across the fields toward St. Davids, out of range of the American artillery. Climbing the heights at a low point near the portage road, he was joined by the Chippawa garrison on top of the escarpment. Sheaffe formed his men in a column and marched toward the American position on top of the heights. More militiamen were sent ahead, including the Coloured Corps, a company of Canadians of African descent, to assist those harassing the entrenched Americans.

A few hundred metres from the American line, now formed on the eastern brow of the heights, Sheaffe moved his men as though on a parade ground, from column to line, spreading them out in a thin line, two men deep. At the order "fix bayonets," 800 men in unison drew their steel bayonets from their leather sheathes and locked them onto their musket barrels. The order was given to advance, and as the drums beat the cadence, the fifes struck up a shrill tune and the men marched slowly together toward the American line. Whenever an American musket ball, wildly inaccurate except at the shortest of range, struck one of the redcoats, the man in the second rank would step forward to fill the gap in the British line. The stately and precise advance of this seemingly unstoppable, well-drilled professional army, whose numbers seemed trebled by the brilliant red of their coats, was enough to intimidate the American soldiers. Less than a hundred paces from the American position, the British line halted. On command, like a machine, their muskets were lowered to the aiming positions and at the word "fire!" the British muskets exploded together in a deafening roll like a clap of thunder. The Americans would have seen the line halt, seen the explosion of the discharge, and

Illustration of the first burial of Brock at Fort George.

then would have completely lost sight of the redcoats, enveloped as they were in the thick white smoke of gunpowder. While few of the British musket balls would have found their targets, the psychological effect of such an explosive attack on untrained soldiers would have been staggering. As the American line reeled under the British musket volley, the smoke began to clear, and through the smoke came the redcoats in a fierce bayonet charge.

The war cries of the charging soldiers were echoed by the militiamen and Native warriors on the American flank. The Americans panicked, but there was nowhere to which they could retreat. Behind them was the steep slope of the escarpment and the swift current of the Niagara River. Many Americans died as they tried to scramble down the escarpment, only to lose their footing and fall to their deaths. Many drowned trying to swim back to Lewiston. The prudent threw down their arms and surrendered. This proved to be somewhat difficult at first. American commander Winfield Scott reported how two men had been sent toward the British with white flags but apparently had been shot down by angry Natives bent on avenging their own losses. Scott, a very tall man at 6'4", finally took a white flag himself, and although fired on several times, was eventually conducted to Sheaffe, who accepted the surrender and eventually organized a cease-fire.

When all was over at about 4:00 in the afternoon, it was clear that this second American invasion had been a dismal failure. A total of 436 American regulars and 489 militiamen

Parks Canada staff in period costume at Brock's Monument, Queenston Heights.

were captured by the British. As many as 500 Americans had been killed or wounded, many by artillery fire at the beginning of the battle, but most because of panic at its conclusion. Of as many as 6,000 men who had gathered at Lewiston, only about 1,600 Americans had fought that day.

On the British side, casualties were lighter. Brock was killed outright and Macdonell mortally wounded. Ten other

British soldiers were killed that day along with two men of the York Militia and as many as eight Six Nations men. Almost 80 men were wounded and some of these died in the days following the battle. Although the losses seem relatively few considering that the battle was fought over a thirteen-hour period at distances of as little as three metres, the loss of Brock was seen as a major blow. He was immediately regarded as the "saviour of Upper Canada," revered by Upper Canadians, and Native Canadians, and admired by his American foes.

A cannon still guards the walls of Fort Erie, which has been restored as a historic site.

Immediately following the battle, Sheaffe arranged an armistice with General Van Rensselaer. Sheaffe offered to send his surgeons to the American lines to help with American wounded, but this offer was politely declined. Brock was honoured with an impressive military funeral and buried in one of the bastions of Fort George. During the funeral procession, the Americans at Fort Niagara fired "minute guns," blank charges in salute to a respected opponent.

The American prisoners captured at Queenston were a problem. The British at Fort George could not arrange enough transport to ship them off to Quebec and did not have sufficient rations to feed them at Fort George for any length of time. Like many of their comrades taken at Detroit, these Americans were offered their "parole." They were allowed to go home in exchange for a solemn promise that they would not take up arms against the British again unless an agreement could be reached releasing a similar number of British from parole. This parole system relied on people keeping their word and made prisoner-of-war camps unnecessary.

For the Americans, Queenston Heights represented another embarrassing defeat. They did learn some valuable lessons, however. They would no longer underestimate the value of well-trained, disciplined soldiers and would only invade again when they had a well-equipped, well-lead, and well-supplied army with soldiers committed to carrying out the invasion and who would not stand on constitutional rights concerning war outside of the United States.

For the British, Queenston Heights and Detroit had shown that the Canadian militia were willing and able to resist an American invasion. The battles also showed the Natives that the British and Canadians would fight, and convinced many young Native men to join in the war against the American invaders. Prior to these actions, Prevost's strategy was to abandon Upper Canada if it was invaded by an overwhelming force, and to concentrate his forces at Quebec. He now realized that the defence of Upper Canada was not only possible but desirable, because the Canadian people would be a major factor in the defence.

American setbacks continued after the Battle of Queenston Heights. Six weeks after this invasion, General Smyth planned to attack the Canadian shore at Fort Erie from Black Rock near Buffalo. He wisely polled his men prior to crossing the river and found that the militia, by and large, still refused to cross to Canadian soil. The attempt was never made.

In the Northwest, other events were afoot which would have a major impact on Native fortunes in the Ohio valley and

Remember the River Raisin! *by Ken Riley depicts the charge of Johnson's mounted infantry against the British 41st Regiment lines.*

River, the American garrison at Ogdensburg, New York, was attacked by a small force of British regulars and Canadian militia who marched across the frozen river on February 22, 1813. The garrison of Ogdensburg, which had conducted a few raids on Canadian soil in the previous weeks, was put to flight. The British captured American cannon and government rations, and the town of Ogdensburg was ransacked primarily by the women of Prescott, the Canadian town across the river from Ogdensburg. It was noted that these women, having been friends with their American neighbours before the war, knew exactly which houses had the most lucrative booty.

British strategy on the Detroit frontier. A new army was being formed by the Americans to replace the force surrendered by Hull at Detroit. Under the leadership of the very talented American general, William Henry Harrison, the army of the Northwest consisted of militia and regulars, with a strong backbone of experienced frontier fighters from Kentucky, Ohio, and Indiana. Harrison set his army in motion in the late autumn, planning to have its three columns converge on Detroit to retake that fort. Once again, though, the Americans suffered a setback when one of the battalions under General Winchester was attacked by a combined British and Native force at Frenchtown (Monroe, Michigan) on the River Raisin. Winchester's troops surrendered, and in the aftermath a number of prisoners were killed. The action became known as a massacre, and "remember the River Raisin" became a rallying cry for the Northwest army in the coming year. While the battle filled Harrison's troops with indignation, it also prevented Harrison from considering an attack on Detroit that winter.

Several hundred kilometres away, on the St. Lawrence

The United States had declared war on Britain in June, and in the next several months faced nothing but embarrassing defeats in the land war. Invasions on the Detroit and Niagara frontiers resulted in disaster, and an intended invasion in the Montreal area could not be organized. The defeat of the Americans in 1812 bought the British more time during which additional forces, weapons, and supplies could be shipped to North America. While the following year would prove a trial for British forces, it was clear that they could gain the upper hand over the Americans, even though outnumbered by the republic's armies. This, of course, depended on the Americans remaining divided on the issue of how to conduct the war and on their continued poor organization and leadership.

The Americans did learn some valuable lessons in the first months of the war, however, and changes were put in motion that would tax the British severely in the coming campaign season. The Americans would regain their lost laurels in 1813 only to lose them again by year's end.

4

The American Capture
of York and Niagara

Control of the Lakes

When the United States of America had declared war on Britain in June 1812, the Americans had gone into war ill-prepared for the defence that would be put up by the British army and Canadian militia with their Native allies. The Americans had poorly organized supply lines, a cumbersome bureaucracy which made it difficult to organize for war, and large armies of new recruits who were poorly trained and badly led. Many of the senior American officers were politically appointed amateurs or aging Revolutionary War veterans who could no longer undertake the rigours of campaign. At the outset of the war, many felt that capturing Canada would involve little more than marching into Upper Canada and then leading the Canadians in a short campaign to throw off the bonds of British rule. On the contrary, however, the Americans found many Canadians fighting tenaciously alongside the British redcoats to drive off the American invaders.

Earthworks covered by cannon made Fort George difficult to attack.

As the year 1812 ended, America was waking up to the realities of the situation. They had learned that they needed a secure, reliable supply system and that they needed to sever the British communications route. The British were able to send troops and supplies from place to place with ease, using the Great Lakes–St. Lawrence transportation routes. By controlling the lakes, the Americans could take control of the land. While this lesson was learned soon after the capture of Detroit in August, it would take some time to prepare fleets on the Great Lakes that could overpower the British naval presence.

Early in the autumn of 1812, Captain Isaac Chauncey of the U.S. Navy was appointed as Commodore of Lakes Ontario and Erie. Prior to Chauncey's arrival at Sackets Harbour on Lake Ontario, the freshwater navy had received very little support from the Navy Department, whose secretary, Paul Hamilton, was not only incompetent but completely ignorant of naval matters.

The U.S. Brig Oneida *off Sackets Harbour, by Peter Rindlisbacher. Although small, the British fleet was sufficient to rule the Great Lakes until U.S. Commodore Chauncey stepped up naval production and launched the* Madison.

In September, President Madison understood that "the command of the lake . . . ought to have been a fundamental part in the national policy" and ordered supplies and sailors to be sent to Sackets Harbour.

Chauncey found only the 16-gun brig *Oneida* and a few converted civilian schooners at Sackets Harbour, kept locked in by the numerically superior British Provincial Marine force, based across Lake Ontario at Kingston. Chauncey purchased several more civilian schooners and armed them with cannon. He also accelerated the building programme at Sackets Harbour so that by late November, the 24-gun corvette *Madison* was launched. In a short time, the Americans felt secure enough to cruise at will on Lake Ontario. During this period, a second shipyard had been established at Presque Isle, Pennsylvania, on Lake Erie, but progress proved slower there.

While Chauncey was strengthening the American lake squadrons, British commander-in-chief Prevost was analysing the Provincial Marine. The Provincial Marine was more of an armed transport service than a naval force and was under the jurisdiction of the Army Commissariat Department. Prevost had Captain Andrew Gray of that department prepare an evaluation of the Provincial Marine in the autumn of 1812, and much was found wanting. Prevost sought help from the Royal Navy, which had a strong presence at Quebec and Halifax, and within a few months, the navy was to take control of the vessels of the Provincial Marine and put the freshwater navy on a more professional footing. A more ambitious building programme was also undertaken, accelerated when reports came back indicating that the new American corvette, *Madison*, was larger and more powerful than the *Royal George*, the largest British vessel then on the lakes.

By April 1813, the Great Lakes were navigable again with the ice having broken up in inland harbours and in the rivers connecting the lakes. In Upper Canada, the British forces were still thinly spread, with forces concentrated at Prescott, Kingston, York, Fort George, Fort Erie, and Detroit. American forces were approaching the Detroit frontier, and were in garrison at Fort Niagara and the Buffalo area, at Oswego, Sackets Harbour, Lake Champlain, and Albany. They were poised to concentrate their troops at any point along the frontier for another invasion which could strike at any place. Prevost remained on the defensive, awaiting the arrival of more troops and supplies to give him enough strength to launch an offensive campaign. The initiative lay with the Americans as it had ten months earlier when war had been declared.

The major differences between June 1812 and April 1813 were that the Americans were better trained by this time, more experienced, better led, and better supplied. The American fleet also temporarily had the upper hand on Lake Ontario. In the spring of 1813, the Americans had a new Secretary of War, John Armstrong, a man with aggressive strategies for finishing the war. He ordered Commodore Chauncey and army commander Major-General Henry Dearborn to cooperate in a campaign to capture Kingston and Niagara and to destroy the defences and shipyard at York.

The Capture of York

York, in early 1813, was the capital of Upper Canada. Known as "muddy York," it was a far cry from the metropolis that Toronto is today. A few streets and avenues had been laid out near the lakeshore, along the harbour west of the Don River, surrounding the legislative buildings, and the dockyard. A lighthouse at Gibraltar Point and a weak cannon battery opposite were the first lines of defence. Fort York, an incomplete earthwork and log fort containing a large magazine for the storage of gunpowder, was the main defensive work with the Governor's residence, barracks, storehouses and a few other government buildings all lying within cannon shot of the fort.

The garrison of York consisted of a few hundred men of the King's 8th Regiment, the Royal Newfoundland Regiment, Glengarry Light Infantry Fencibles, and the York Militia. There were also a few dozen dockyard workers busy constructing a new vessel for the Lake Ontario fleet. General Sheaffe, still in command in Upper Canada, had alerted Prevost of the weakness of York's defences and suggested that the Americans would attack in the spring, but little was done to improve the situation. When the Americans did strike,

Fort York, 1805, *by S. Stretton. When the Americans attacked in 1813, the garrison had only a few hundred soldiers and militiamen to defend it.*

Toronto, 1813, *by Owen Staples. The American invading force included more than 1,700 men and 15 ships.*

Sheaffe had only 700 men to undertake the defence of York.

On the afternoon of April 26, 1813, lookouts on the Scarborough bluffs reported that sails were in sight on the lake, heading toward York. As the vessels slowly clawed their way toward them, the men in the Gibraltar Point lighthouse were able to count 15 craft, the vessels of Chauncey's American fleet. On board were 1,700 American troops under the command of Brigadier Zebulon Pike, the noted explorer, after whom Pike's Peak in Colorado is named. The expedition was under the overall command of General Henry Dearborn, who was to watch the unfolding drama from Chauncey's flagship.

Sheaffe was at a disadvantage. With few cannon mounted at York, the American ships could sail at will along the harbour and could land troops anywhere. Sheaffe anticipated that they would land beyond his western battery, and dispatched a company of Glengarry Fencibles and a few Mississauga allies to that point, while keeping his main force in reserve at the fort. On the morning of April 27, when the Americans began their invasion, they outflanked this small force of Glengarries and Natives, established a bridgehead,

and were able to land a number of troops. The Native warriors were able to push through the woods to snipe at the Americans, but the Glengarries became tangled in the woods or lost. The Grenadier Company of the King's 8th Regiment was sent to oppose the American landing, and although they mounted a brave bayonet charge, which temporarily drove back four times their own number of enemy soldiers toward the beach, these men were continually bombarded by the cannon of Chauncey's fleet and suffered heavy casualties. Eventually, they were forced to retreat as more Americans landed and joined the fight. British and Canadian troops were hastily dispatched to the landing site, but arrived in small groups, which were easily driven off by the enemy.

Soon the Americans were able to land field guns and form their troops to march on York's defences. As they approached the western battery behind which many of the British soldiers had retreated, the guns of the battery fired at the Americans and at their ships. Whether as a result of counter fire by the Americans or a costly mistake by one of the British gunners, the battery's small powder magazine exploded in a ball of fire, killing a score of men outright and hideously burning others.

The Americans quickly overran the ruins of that battery and prepared to advance on Fort York.

In the three hours since the American landing, Sheaffe's men had suffered severely, with at least 62 killed and 94 wounded, while other troops remained scattered in the woods. Fort York was poorly armed, and Sheaffe had perhaps as few as 400 defenders remaining with which to try and stop an American force of over 1,400, supported by field guns and the cannon of the American fleet. Regular troops were a precious commodity and Sheaffe had no choice but to retreat toward Kingston to save the remnants of his army, abandoning York to its fate. He ordered the new ship being built in the York shipyard, the *Sir Isaac Brock*, to be burned along with the naval storehouse and had a fuse lit to explode the large quantity of gunpowder in Fort York's powder magazine.

As the British force retreated on the Kingston road, leaving the scene of action through a ravine by the back gate of Fort York, and as the American army continued to advance, the main magazine at Fort York exploded with devastating force. Witnesses described a mushroom cloud that could be seen from as far away as Fort Niagara. The sound of the explosion was heard at Fort George. The force of the explosion shattered most of the windows of the houses in York and showered the area with stone debris. General Pike, several hundred metres from the magazine at the time of the explosion, was mortally wounded when struck by one of the large chunks of rock that came raining down following the blast. Thirty-eight American soldiers were killed in the explosion while 222 were wounded, many severely.

York was now in American hands, but at a heavy cost, 55 having been killed and 265 wounded during the foray. They stayed for a few days and seized what government stores they could, including a number of cannon that were to be sent on to bolster the defences of Fort George. The Americans did some looting of private property and burned the government buildings in the town. They then reboarded their ships and sailed back toward American territory, planning to get back to Niagara and launch a surprise attack on Fort George, but they were delayed off Gibraltar Point by adverse winds.

At Fort Niagara on the New York side of the Niagara River, the American garrison anxiously awaited news of the attack on York. They knew that the fleet was landing an invasion force there and had seen and heard the explosion of the powder magazine, but had noted that the fleet was

Officers' Mess at Fort York, which has recently completed a restoration. (Inset) Interior of Officers' Mess.

View of Fort Niagara, by Henri Beau.

The Battle of Fort George

On May 21, 1813, Chauncey's fleet returned to the mouth of the Niagara River after delivering more reinforcements to Fort Niagara. There were now over 8,000 American soldiers on the Niagara frontier. The Americans had also assembled numerous barges, boats, and bateaux, enough to move their entire army. A few hundred metres away, across the Niagara river, the garrisons of Fort George and Queenston, under the command of British Brigadier-General John Vincent, remained alert and apprehensive. Vincent's army, guarding an 18-kilometre front, consisted of 1,050 regulars of the Royal Artillery, the King's 8th, the Royal Newfoundland Fencible Regiment, the Glengarry Light Infantry Fencibles, and the 41st and 49th regiments. He also had 300 militiamen from Lincoln County, 88 artificers or tradesmen, and 28 men of the Coloured Corps. About 50 Six Nations warriors, ready to help, were camped nearby. Vincent was outnumbered by at least eight to one.

The artillery mounted in and about Fort George was inadequate. Guns intended for the fort had been captured at York in April and were now in American hands. On the Canadian shore were seven heavy cannons, mostly short-range "carronades," five lighter guns including three mobile field pieces, two heavy mortars, five light mortars, and a small howitzer.

late in returning to Niagara as planned. Finally, General Dearborn and his staff were able to reach Niagara on May 3. The wounded arrived the following day to be joined soon afterwards by the main body of troops carried by the rest of the fleet. One young American officer described the pitiful wounds of those caught in the explosion of the magazine at York. These men had been aboard ship for close to a week before they finally disembarked at Fort Niagara and were placed in a makeshift barracks hospital. "Seldom has a hospital exhibited such a spectacle of misery. Such was the mashing effect of it [the explosion], that the human form often lost all its distinctive characteristics, and looked like a shapeless mass of livid bloatedness."

With the losses at York, the shock of the explosion, and the delay in the return of Chauncey's fleet and Dearborn's army to Niagara, combined with the fact that the British did not strip the garrison of Fort George to counterattack at York, the Americans decided to alter their original plan to immediately assault Fort George. More troops were wanted at Niagara, and Chauncey's fleet returned to Sackets Harbour to prepare to attack Fort George at a later date, after better preparations had been made.

Field artillery at Fort George, with the Blockhouse in the background.

Scott's Capture of Fort George, *artist unknown. Backed up by 25 guns at Ft. Niagara and over 90 cannon on Chauncey's fleet, the Americans pounded Ft. George into submission in May of 1813.*

In cannon batteries at Fort Niagara and directly across the river at Youngstown's "Salt" Battery, the Americans had over twenty-five guns and mortars, most with longer ranges than Fort George's guns. While the artillery available to both sides was more or less equal in destructive capability, the Americans had the added firepower of Chauncey's fleet, over 90 cannon including the 26 heavy, long range guns on the American ship *General Pike*.

At daybreak on May 25, the American artillery opened fire on Fort George. Hundreds of heavy cannonballs tore through the wooden palisades, earthen ramparts, and log buildings of the fort. Shells fired from American mortars exploded in and around the fortification, blasting earth and parts of the fort's buildings into the sky. Red-hot iron shell fragments whizzed through the air, cutting down anyone caught in the open. Some of these exploding shells weighed over 45 kilograms and went off with a terrific blast when their fuse reached the explosive charge of the shell. Finally, "hot shot" (cannonballs heated red-hot) set Fort George's buildings on fire. By day's end, the cannon at Fort George had been silenced and all of the buildings of the fort burned — except the fort's vulnerable powder magazine and other storage areas dug into the earthworks. An infantry assault was now expected and Vincent posted troops along the river and Lake Ontario at likely landing spots.

The powder magazine at Fort George.

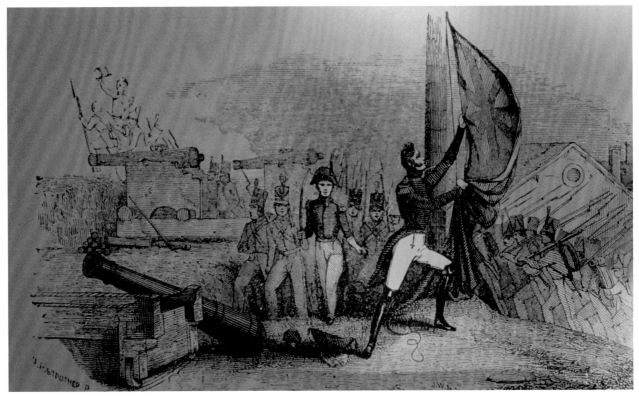

To the shame of the British, the Americans captured the Union Jack along with the fort. The flag could not be lowered prior to the retreat, as its mast had been broken during the fort's bombardment.

Little happened the following day. The log buildings of Fort George had been reduced to smoking embers. The garrison stood ready, watching for movement on the American shore, but no invasion was launched that day. The Americans relaxed in their sprawling camp four miles further along the American shore of Lake Ontario, out of site and range of the Canadian shore. Their commanding officer, Major-General Morgan Lewis, ensured that everything was ready for the invasion: ammunition and rations were issued, militiamen were committed to the enterprise, officers were briefed, and the navy was ready.

At 1:00 a.m., the American troops began to march down to the waiting boats and within two hours began forming into three columns of boats guarded by the ships of the navy. The manoeuvre, performed on a dark night and in a heavy fog, was masterful, showing brilliant organization and leadership.

On the Canadian shore, small groups of British and Canadian troops, lying in the open on that chilly, damp May morning, could clearly hear the sounds of oars in the boats of the invasion force, the rattle of equipment, the squeal of ropes in pulleys, and the flap of sails as the American boats and ships set sail, but they could see nothing through the dense fog that covered Lake Ontario. Just before daybreak, the air was shattered by the roar of artillery as the Americans again began to bombard the ruins of Fort George. Through gaps in the fog, the British could now see the sails of American ships, heading toward the shore between Mississauga Point and the Two Mile Creek.

Canadian cannon batteries at Mississauga Point and Two Mile Creek opened fire as the American invasion craft became visible, rowing toward shore in three columns. The small batteries were blasted away by the American ships covering the

When the British recaptured Ft. George, they built Ft. Mississauga to help defend it.

landing. The first American boats grated ashore and infantrymen poured forth, assembling on the beach before scaling the small sand cliff that overlooked the shore. A squad of men of the Glengarry Light Infantry Regiment, with men of the Coloured Corps and Six Nations warriors who had been posted near the landing place, raced to the top of the bank to fire down on the American landing force. The guns of Chauncey's fleet opened fire with solid cannonballs and the deadly grape shot, which "so completely enfiladed and scoured the plains that it became impossible to approach the beach."

The American advance force, 800 men of the elite Forsythe's Rifle Regiment and the flank companies of the 15th Infantry, supported by light artillery, all under the talented American Colonel Winfield Scott, touched shore and the fleet ceased firing. On the Canadian shore, the 470 defenders rushed forward to the lakeshore to fire at the American force that had just landed, pushing them back below the embankment to the lake's edge. Again the American cannon opened fire. Grape-shot and musket balls, thick as hail, flailed across the field over which the British advanced. Once more they retreated, and the Americans stopped firing their cannon to allow their infantry to advance. The British and Canadian defenders, reduced by heavy casualties, again drove the growing invasion army back. The ships reopened fire, severely reducing the British ranks.

Scott's advance force was joined by the 6th and 16th regiments and the remainder of the 15th Regiment, and finally Scott stood above the embankment with about 2,300 men. The British and Canadian force was joined by the men of the 49th, but now stood at less than 600. They nevertheless formed in a battle line. According to American General Boyd, who had arrived on the scene at this time, the two sides spent

a quarter of an hour exchanging volleys at a distance of "only six or ten yards."

As more Americans landed and began to outflank the small force of defenders, the British wisely decided to fall back toward Fort George. They continued to resist, standing to engage the advancing Americans near the Presbyterian Church and on the Commons by the fort, but they finally realized that all was lost. Fuses were lit leading to the small ammunition magazines dug into the earthworks of Fort George, the cannon were spiked, and the force retreated up the road toward Queenston. They could not take the Union Jack which flew over the fort with them. The American artillery bombardment had been so fierce that the halyards of the flag staff had been severed by cannonballs. Normally, it was considered a great dishonour to have your flag captured by the enemy, but in this case the British had no choice but to abandon it.

Casualties at the Battle of Fort George had been very heavy. The Americans reported 39 killed and 111 wounded. The first official British report listed 52 killed, 45 wounded, and 262 "wounded and missing" among the regulars in action. This figure did not include Native warriors and Canadian militia. At least eight militiamen were killed and ten wounded, two of whom later died from their wounds. It is difficult to determine how many men lie buried where they fell on the field of battle that day. The Americans claimed that there were 108 British and Canadian dead on the field, 163 wounded prisoners, and 115 unwounded prisoners.

Stoney Creek and Beaver Dams, June 1813

Monument at Smith's Knoll, Stoney Creek.

Following the Battle of Fort George on May 27, the American army occupied the frontier from Lake Ontario to Lake Erie. Their bridgehead at Fort George was intended to be a springboard to the conquest of Upper Canada. First they had to defeat the small British force which had retreated to Burlington Heights, where

Six Nations warriors escort Laura Secord past enemy lines to Fizgibbon at Decew House. Painting by Henry Sandham.

knew that his small force at Burlington Heights would not be able to withstand a well-planned assault by the much larger American force. Luckily, he was a daring officer — a man of action. On June 5, 1813, his small force advanced toward Stoney Creek where the Americans had stopped for the night. He instructed his men to remove the flints from their muskets to ensure that no one could accidentally fire one, and then in the pitch-black early hours of June 6, his force attacked the American camp at bayonet point. The fighting was confused, and the British had to withdraw before dawn lest the Americans see how small the numbers of British were and rally to defeat them. In the end, the British captured both American generals and plunged the American army into confusion and disorganization, forcing them to retreat to Fort George.

Beginning with small forces of Native warriors, Vincent sent increasing numbers of men to the vicinity of Fort George to observe and harass the American troops there. Soldiers leaving the safety of the fort to gather provisions, fodder, or firewood were ambushed in the woods surrounding Fort George. American intelligence showed that one of the centres of this guerilla force was near Beaver Dams at the Decew house. An army of over 500 men under General Boyd was sent from the fort to destroy this depot. Stopping at Queenston en route, they discussed their plans. They were overheard by Queenston resident Laura Secord, who set off to warn James Fitzgibbon, the young officer in command at Decew's. Fitzgibbon in turn asked his Native allies to remain watchful.

The movements of the American army were watched carefully by scouts from the Seven Nations of Lower Canada, mostly Iroquoian people. Near Beaver Dams,

Dundurn Castle now stands in Hamilton. The British had a small defensive work on this height, and set about strengthening the position.

Meanwhile, the Americans prepared to wipe out this last British force in the area. A large force under Generals Winder and Chandler left Fort George to advance up the road to Burlington Heights. British commander General Vincent

an ambush was laid. The Americans stumbled into it on June 24, and were forced to surrender to Fitzgibbon after being pinned down by Native gunfire. The Battle of Beaver Dams was an important victory, causing the Americans to overestimate the number of British, Canadians, and Natives controlling the woods around Niagara. They would remain isolated in Fort George during the remainder of the year, and were never able to exploit their toehold on Canadian soil. The Americans strengthened the defences at Fort George, extending a trench and palisade as far as the Anglican Church and down to the river, creating a large fortified camp. Sentry stations or "piquets" were established at various points within a mile of the fort, based at various residences that the Americans had commandeered — the McFarland, Secord, and Butler homesteads.

The British, now confident after Stoney Creek and Beaver Dams, advanced as far as Four Mile Creek, where they set up several fortified camps. They were now under the command of Major-General de Rottenburg, an expert in light infantry tactics. They reoccupied Queenston and established a head-quarters at St. Davids.

Once established on the Four Mile Creek, the British army, Canadian militia, and Native warriors began to make life very uncomfortable for the American army of occupation at Niagara. Ambushes were sprung on troops heading to relieve the advanced piquets or out foraging for firewood or fodder. Native warriors or troops would stealthily approach the American outposts at night, take cover, prepare their muskets, and make noise. When nervous American sentries would shout "Who goes there?" the concealed men would fire at the voice, wounding many American sentries and killing some in the process.

Whipping in the Americans: The Summer and Autumn of 1813

Detail of a flintlock musket.

Throughout the summer of 1813, the British maintained a siege of the American positions in and around Fort George. They continued to annoy the Americans by ambush and by sporadic attacks on the outlying American strongpoints. One American officer said that these "piquet alarms occurred about as often as our meals."

On July 8, a more serious attack against the American piquets was launched. William Hamilton Merritt of the Provincial Light Dragoons led a group of British regulars and a few wagons to retrieve medicines and surgical instruments that had been hidden at Cassel Corus's farm on the Black Swamp Road (Regional Road 55) when the Americans captured Niagara on May 27. While the medicines were being recovered, a force of Six Nations warriors under John Norton and 60 Mississaugas and Ottawas under Blackbird, moved toward the Butler homestead, where one American piquet was stationed. Norton's scouts informed him that the Americans had sent a force of 200 infantry and cavalry in advance of the

British infantry with Native scout, portrayed by Fort George staff.

Red Jacket of the Seneca.

piquet position in the vicinity of Ball's farm. The Americans were planning to outflank the British wagons on the Black Swamp Road. Norton deployed his men into the woods to lay an ambush, but his men fired too soon and alerted the enemy. The Americans advanced more cautiously, and Norton retreated to try to entice the Americans into another ambush hastily planned further in the woods. The Americans launched a cavalry charge toward the Natives, but swung away before reaching the woods where the Natives had positioned themselves. The American infantry would not approach closer than 300 yards, too great a distance for musket fire to be effective. Encouraged, the Natives advanced toward them, driving the American infantry back toward Butler's farm.

The Americans had been training for just such an action. They had laid plans to have mobile forces in readiness to outflank any British attacks on their piquets. On this day, Lieutenant Eldridge of the 13th U.S. Infantry led as many as 90 men to move on the edge of Butler's farm to attack the flank of Norton's force. Norton saw the advancing force and retreated deeper into the woods, pursued by Eldridge's men. The Natives were able to prevent Eldridge's retreat and, in a quick skirmish, killed or captured all of Eldridge's men. Eldridge himself was killed when he shot a young Native after apparently surrendering.

While the smoke from Eldridge's defeat still hung in the woods, a larger contingent of American infantry advanced to the scene. By this time, the wagon loads of retrieved medicines had reached the safety of the British lines, and the Natives melted away into the forest, returning to the safety of the British positions. The relieving American force discovered only the dead and dying on Butler's and Ball's fields. Between 20 and 30 Americans were buried where they fell.

The action at Butler's farm forced the Americans to be even more cautious. Morale collapsed and the American troops at the piquets became nervous. The British and Canadians and their Native allies continued to keep the Americans bottled up at Fort George. American General Peter Porter, on arrival at Fort George, described the situation in a letter to the Secretary of War, reporting that the army at Fort George, even though it outnumbered the British surrounding it, "lies panic-struck — shut up, and whipped in by a few hundred miserable Savages, leaving the whole of this frontier, excepting the mile in extent which we occupy, exposed to the inroads & depredations of the enemy."

A few days after the action at Butler's farm, the British again took the initiative to further unbalance the Americans. On July 11, a force of British regulars and militia crossed the Niagara River to raid the American artillery position at Black Rock. They captured weapons and stores, burned the military buildings at the site, and retreated back to the Canadian shore. The Americans now felt unsafe on both sides of the river.

The Americans had more than enemy action to fear. Poor camp sanitation and atrocious personal hygiene among the American forces were taking their toll. Dysentry and "lake fever" kept the hospitals full, and dozens died of disease while camped at Fort George. Similarly, although the British and Canadians were extremely careful about their camp sanitation and were considered at the time

Camp kitchen at a re-enactment.

The Laura Secord Homestead. (Inset) The kitchen inside Laura Secord Homestead.

to be fanatical about personal hygiene, we may well wonder at their standards in these areas. Soldiers were required to wash head, hands, and feet each morning, but no arrangements were made for full-body bathing. They also suffered from fevers and dysentery, but not as severely as did the Americans. While half of the Americans at Fort George were on the sick list, a third of the British in the area were ill.

Meanwhile, the war against the American piquets continued. On July 17, the Natives again ambushed an American force on its way to relieve one of their piquets. It is claimed that they killed as many as 45 and captured 16 others in this action.

The Americans soon received a boost to their morale with the arrival in mid-July of a party of Oneida and Seneca warriors from New York State. On July 18, these warriors first saw action, outwitting some British dragoons and firing on some of the Native allies under Norton.

On Lake Ontario, the Americans had again achieved the upper hand, and on July 31 they made an attempt on Burlington, followed by a landing at York where the army destroyed Government buildings and left on August 3. By mid-August, the Americans were confident enough to turn the tables on the British near Fort George. On August 16, the Americans attacked one of the British piquets near Ball's farm, and although they did not overrun the position, the skirmish resulted in several British deaths.

A week later, General Sir George Prevost, commander-in-chief of the British forces in Canada, arrived at St. Davids to see at first hand the situation on the Niagara frontier. At his command were 2,883 British regulars and Canadian militia. On August 24, Prevost ordered a comprehensive attack on all five of the American sentry posts, which were fortified at the homesteads of Crooks, Secord, Johnson Butler, Thomas Butler, and McClellan. This was to be a "reconnaissance in force" to test the defences of Fort George. The Americans in the outposts were driven back to Fort George, and some of the British were able to enter the town. Many officers wanted to push on to capture the fort, but Prevost was an extremely cautious man and drew his force back after driving off the American sentries and getting a close look at Fort George. Fort George was still in American hands, but it was clear that the British had regained the initiative on the Niagara frontier.

5

Montreal Saved: The Battles of Chateauguay and Crysler's Farm

On February 5, 1813, John Armstrong was appointed as the United States Secretary of War, taking over from the ineffectual William Eustis, who had left the office in December 1812. Armstrong developed a strategy which involved three main thrusts, the objectives being the retaking of the Detroit frontier by General William Henry Harrison, the capture of York, Niagara, and Kingston, and finally the capture of Montreal. The main effort was to be the capture of Montreal, which would cut off the entire interior of Canada. The capture of the other strongpoints would allow the Americans to defeat the British Army in detail, prevent the reinforcement of Montreal, neutralize the Royal Navy on Lakes Erie and Ontario, and ensure that the American flanks and supply lines were protected.

One objective of the overall campaign had been partially achieved with the capture of York and the invasion of Niagara under Major-General Henry Dearborn assisted by the American navy under Commodore Chauncey. However, York had not been held and Niagara had proven a millstone, tying down a besieged American army in the fort as the British forces on that frontier continued to increase. Armstrong realized that the British had few forces to concentrate at any point, and with the British reinforcing Niagara, the Detroit frontier and either Kingston or Montreal would be weakly held. By early autumn, the time seemed right to strike at these objectives.

Battle of Lake Erie, *by Peter Rindlisbacher.*

The Battle of Lake Erie and Defeat at Moraviantown

While William Henry Harrison's army slowly gathered on the Detroit frontier (in spite of forays by British General Proctor and Native allies under the war chief, Tecumseh), the Americans could make little headway as long as the British controlled Lake Erie with their Amherstburg-based fleet. For the past year, however, the Americans had been labouriously hauling timber, iron, canvas, rope, cannon, and heavy anchors to their small shipyard near Erie, Pennsylvania. By late August, American Commodore Oliver Hazzard Perry had a fleet to match that of the Royal Navy on Lake Erie.

Battle of Lake Erie, *by J.C.H. Forster. The British set out to decimate the American fleet, but ended up being captured themselves at Put-in-Bay.*

On September 9, 1813, the British garrison at Amherstburg was isolated and poorly supplied thanks to the American control of Fort George. Food was in particularly short supply. The British squadron on Lake Erie had ships as good as those of the Americans, including a new ship, the *Detroit*, but the ships were very poorly armed and had few trained sailors to man the sails and guns. Nonetheless, British Captain Robert Barclay sailed out to try to destroy Perry's fleet. He needed to control the lake to pick up supplies awaiting him at the other end of it. The alternative was to sit at Amherstburg and starve.

The two fleets met on September 10 near Put-in-Bay, Ohio, and while the British dominated the action at first, heavy casualties stripped their ships of their experienced seamen and officers, and soon Perry's American fleet gained the upper hand. By the end of the day, the entire British squadron had been captured. Perry sent off a memorable dispatch summarizing his feat: "We have met the enemy and they are ours."

At Amherstburg, Proctor and Tecumseh and their men heard the distant gunfire, and knew that a battle was taking place across the lake, but they had to anxiously await word of the outcome. They finally learned of Barclay's defeat and faced a grim decision. Proctor realized that he was completely cut off, with Fort George in American hands, Lake Erie now an American pond, Harrison's army advancing, and no prospect of receiving reinforcements. He decided to abandon Detroit and Fort Malden and to retreat up the Thames River. From there, he would continue to Burlington Heights, the headquarters of the British Army of the Centre, which was concentrating here to continue the war on the Niagara frontier. Tecumseh wanted to hold the forts, to fight to the death rather than give ground. In the end, however, Tecumseh and his supporters followed Proctor's army.

The American army was able to cross easily to the Canadian shore on Perry's ships. Detroit was quickly reoccupied, and Harrison's army soon arrived at Amherstburg and Fort Malden but found that the British had torched all of the military buildings and the adjacent shipyard. Harrison's

Battle of the Thames *(or Moraviantown), by J.C.H. Forster.*

army set off in pursuit of the retreating British garrison and finally overtook Proctor and Tecumseh on the Thames River near the settlement of Moraviantown on October 5, 1813. After a brief but fierce struggle, Harrison won the Battle of Moraviantown. Proctor and part of his army were able to withdraw safely, and eventually made it to Burlington Heights. Tecumseh was slain and his Native army dispersed, some following Proctor to Burlington but most returning many miles to their homes. The Detroit frontier was now firmly in American hands.

Word reached the British forces on the Niagara frontier in September that the Lake Erie fleet had been captured by the Americans, and on October 7, they received reports of the defeat of the Right Division of the army at the Battle of the Thames two days earlier. False reports of the total destruction of the Right Division and of a large American army advancing from the west forced the British to abandon their positions at Niagara and retire to Burlington Heights. The army of the Centre, commanded by General de Rottenburg, decided to abandon Niagara, and orders were actually given to begin the retreat to Kingston.

On learning that the rumours of the action of October 5 were greatly exaggerated, however, the British cancelled the orders to retreat, continued to strengthen their position at Burlington Heights, and sent large patrols toward Niagara. In November, they learned that the American garrison of Fort George had been greatly reduced to reinforce an army under James Wilkinson, which was planning an attack on Montreal.

While the first of Armstrong's objectives had gone well for the Americans, the main objective, Montreal, was to prove the downfall of the American hopes of 1813.

Chateauguay

American strategists realized that they would not be able to conquer Upper Canada without achieving naval control of Lake Ontario. Chauncey had not been able to bring the British to bay, for as he continued to build his fleet at Sackets Harbour, the Royal Navy under Commodore James Lucas Yeo was matching him in the arms race by building increasingly larger vessels at Kingston. The need to capture Kingston and destroy the dockyard, thus depriving Yeo of his base, seemed like the obvious next move. With the British amassing at Niagara, they could not defend both Montreal and Kingston.

The American plan was to assemble an army on Lake Champlain under Major-General Wade Hampton to threaten Montreal, while another army under Major-General James Wilkinson would assemble at Sackets Harbour to attack Kingston. The strategy was sound. If the British stripped Montreal to reinforce Kingston, Hampton would be able to attack Montreal. If the British kept their forces at Montreal to meet Hampton's threat, Kingston would remain weak and Wilkinson could easily capture the fort and dockyard. The flaw in the strategy was in the choice of generals and in the lack of training for the bulk of their armies.

Major-General James Wilkinson, assembling an army at Sackets Harbour, developed a slightly different plan. Rather than attacking Kingston directly, he had a more ambitious agenda, outlined in his letter of August 20, 1813: "To rendezvous the whole of the troops on the lake in this vicinity ... to make a bold feint upon Kingston ... and in concert with the division under MajorGeneral Hampton to take Montreal." Hampton, who apparently detested Wilkinson and would take no direction from him, followed his own council based on Armstrong's original plans.

On September 19, Hampton crossed the Canadian border at Odelltown with an army of 4,000 infantry, 200 cavalry, and ten pieces of artillery. The intended route was more difficult than anticipated, with few sources of fresh water along the way. Hampton

An aerial view of Fort Henry as it appears today. The fort guards the harbour at Kingston. (Inset) The advanced battery at modern-day Fort Henry.

changed his route, returning to the American side of the border and marching 60 kilometres west to a point along the Chateauguay, a river that flowed eventually into the St. Lawrence upriver from Montreal. On learning of this move, the British mustered a force of regulars supported by Lower Canadian militia to counter Hampton's manoeuvres. Major-General de Watteville was placed in command of British and Canadian army opposing this threat, while Major-General Roger Hale Sheaffe was placed in command of the reserve forces that could be sent to any threatened point.

When the Americans discovered that the British were quickly mustering a very mobile force under de Rottenburg, Hampton was ordered to advance with speed to the mouth of the Chateauguay on the St. Lawrence, to prevent the British from reinforcing Kingston. On October 21, the American army again crossed into Canada along the Chateauguay River.

In the meantime, Lieutenant-Colonel Charles de Salaberry,

a Canadian-born officer in the British army, was preparing defences on the banks of the Chateauguay to slow down the American advance. His men built several lines of defences on the west bank of the river — trenches guarded by abatis, made of sharpened tree branches, then placed facing the direction of the enemy's advance. Manning the first line of defence were 150 Canadian Voltigeurs who had been specially trained in light infantry tactics. There were also 50 men of the Canadian Fencible Infantry Regiment, 100 Lower Canadian "Sedentary Militia" who had some training, but who were basically amateurs in arms, and some Native warriors. Another 160 militia were stationed on the east bank of the river to guard a ford through shallow water. Two thousand metres to the rear of these positions were the reserve of 300 Voltigeurs, 200 sedentary militia, 150 Native warriors, and 480 well-trained "Select Embodied" militia, all under the command of the fiery Lieutenant-Colonel "Red" George Macdonell of the Glengarry Light Infantry Fencible Regiment.

Col. Charles de Salaberry.

On October 25, Hampton's scouts discovered the small force behind the first line of de Salaberry's defences and greatly underestimated the strength of the British position. Hampton was able to learn about the ford and ordered Colonel Purdy of the U.S. Army to take 1,500 men along the east side of the river to cross at the ford and come at de Salaberry's defences from the rear. He would then advance on the British with the rest of the army in a frontal attack along the west bank.

In the late morning of October 26, Purdy's army advanced, and when opposite de Salaberry's position the Americans came under fire from the west bank on their flank. They pushed on toward the ford but soon came under heavy fire from the militiamen stationed there to defend it. They also saw that there was more to the British position than de Salaberry's small force. They became aware of Macdonell's larger reserve force a little farther downriver. Panic set in, and the American army, consisting primarily of raw troops, began to withdraw.

At the same time, Hampton's main force had become entangled in the abatis of de Salaberry's defences, and the men were suffering heavy casualties as a result of the concentrated fire from the small Canadian force opposing them. Over 50 men had been hit by accurate fire, while the Canadians suffered half that number of casualties. Hampton also became aware of the reserve force under Macdonell. That force, dimly seen through the thick woods, was made to seem even larger as the Canadians shouted orders, screamed war cries, and blew signals on their bugles, the notes of which echoed through the woods. The 1,500 men in de Salaberry's and Macdonell's forces were estimated to be several times that number by the nervous Americans. Hampton gave the signal, and on both sides of the Chateauguay, the American force, which still had over 3,500 men, retreated — much to the relief of de Salaberry, who had only 339 men involved in the battle.

Hampton took his army back to Chateauguay, New York. The skirmish had not caused very many casualties in the American force, which still stood at over 4,000 men, but Hampton realized that these men were frightened, demoralized, and untrained. Also, the weather was dismal, and winter was approaching. The number of British forces between his army and Montreal was greatly overestimated, and so Hampton resolved to retire to winter quarters, deciding against an attack on Montreal in that year. In doing so, he also decided not to proceed to the St. Lawrence to reinforce Wilkinson.

Crysler's Farm

While Hampton's army was approaching the Chateauguay River and de Salaberry finishing his defences, General Prevost had dispatched reinforcements to Kingston to counter the threat posed by Wilkinson's American army, which was now ready to move from Sackets Harbour. Wilkinson set off with his army of 8,000 men on October 17. They were loaded in every boat that he could buy or build, and slowly advanced down the St. Lawrence. For two weeks they had to take refuge in the protected bays of the Thousand Islands while an autumn storm brought rain and choppy waters, which threatened to upset his boats, but on November 5 he was on the move once more.

As soon as it became clear that Kingston was not the object of Wilkinson's campaign, British Lieutenant-Colonel Joseph Morrison of the 89th Regiment was ordered to take 450 men of his regiment, 160 men of the 49th Regiment, and two field guns on board bateaux and gunboats to follow the American army and harass them during their descent of the river. His force was considered a "corps of observation," which would keep an eye on all of the American moves so that there would be no surprises, and to slow the American advance.

Within a few days, Wilkinson's army was near Ogdensburg, New York, at the head of a set of rapids in the St. Lawrence and opposite the new British Fort Wellington, in Prescott. Wilkinson disembarked his men, marching them overland south of Ogdensburg and out of cannon range of the fort. The boats, empty of all but their crews, were floated down the river at night, but nonetheless came under a heavy bombardment by the guns of Fort Wellington. While the boats and crews descended unimpaired, a number of British cannonballs crashed through houses in the American town, terrifying the citizens.

Downriver from Prescott, Wilkinson reboarded most of his army, preparing to shoot the rapids above the Canadian town of Iroquois. Increasing numbers of Canadian militia had been sniping at the Americans, and Wilkinson ordered an American force of 2,500 men under Brigadier-General Jacob Brown to cross to the Canadian side to drive away the militia and guard against the force under Morrison, which he knew was following. Wilkinson didn't want to be attacked while in the vulnerable position of descending the rapids, as his men would not be able to fire back at any harassing troops on shore. The American advance continued slowly and cautiously.

Morrison's "corps of observation" arrived at Prescott on November 9, and was joined by an additional 240 men including regulars of the 49th Regiment and the well-trained

men of the Canadian Fencibles and Canadian Voltigeurs. The local militia, with a field gun and some mounted troopers of Fraser's Troop of the Provincial Light Dragoons, joined the march, and together they set off downriver to continue to close in on Wilkinson's army. Morrison now had a force of 900 men with which to harass the 8,000 men of the American invasion force.

On November 10, the Americans reached the Canadian town of Williamsburg and set up camp downriver. Morrison's force arrived in the area at the same time and took up a position on rising ground behind two large ravines in the fields of John Crysler's farm. Soldiers from both sides shivered around their fires that night, able to see the fires of their enemies across the muddy fields.

On the morning of November 11, Wilkinson decided to deal with Morrison's force with half his army before ascending

A detail from the Crysler's Farm Mural at the Crysler's Farm Battlefield Memorial.

Crysler's Farm Monument, near Upper Canada Village.

Cannon at Crysler's Farm Monument.

were grey, and the great-coated regulars, were all untrained militia. At that time, many American militiamen, who were notorious for their lack of training, dressed in grey coats. The Americans underestimated the professionalism of the troops facing them and could easily see how few were their numbers. With little in the form of a tactical plan, the Americans attacked.

The Battle of Crysler's Farm was the type of battle in which the smooth bore musket could be used to its greatest effect and in which British linear tactics proved superior. During the two-hour battle, American regiments would drive at the thin British line, firing from a distance, dropping down on one knee to reload, advancing pell-mell, losing their formation, and causing few casualties to the British as they neared the red and grey ranks. The British held their fire until the Americans were within metres of their line, and then fired devastating volleys into the clumps of American infantry. The survivors retreated in disorder as another group rushed the British line.

Early in the battle, an American force marched through the woods, driving off the Canadian defenders and threatening the left flank of the British line. The men of the 89th Regiment on this flank performed a precise parade-square type of manoeuvre, a left backwards wheel, quickly and efficiently marching into a position to face this American threat. Precise volleys of musket fire soon drove off the attackers in a state of disorder. At the same time, the main American advance, accompanied by mounted dragoons, attacked directly across the field and first ravine, only to be driven back by artillery fire and the musketry of the well-drilled 49th Regiment.

As the Americans moved back, Morrison ordered a general advance, and the regulars slowly marched in step toward the

the Long Sault, a very treacherous set of rapids that made river travel a challenge. He dispatched more men to the Canadian shore and gave orders for an attack on the British position. He did not want his men harassed while descending the rapids and felt that half of his force was more than enough to destroy the British force under Morrison. Wilkinson himself did not take the field, having been very ill since the beginning of the campaign.

Morrison dispatched his militia, Fencibles, and some Native warriors who had joined him, into the woods north of Crysler's Farm, while a unit of British regulars and Canadian fencibles manned the area between the two ravines. British gunboats, which had kept pace with Morrison's force, sat in the river opposite the British position. Morrison divided his regulars into two sections and the men formed up "in line," two men deep in a line from the river to the woods with the river flank covered by the gunboats.

Although the bedridden Wilkinson continued to send orders to his army, the command of the men in the field was confused. Finally, Brigadier-General John Boyd took command. The Americans began the attack on Morrison's position in the early afternoon. Half of the British regulars were in their red coats while the others had their winter grey great-coats covering their red coatees. The Americans assumed that the well-trained Canadian Voltigeurs, whose uniforms

The American Landing at Crysler's Farm, *by Peter Rindlisbacher.*

American horde. The American artillery opened fire, but the British charged their guns. The British advance was checked, but they advanced again. The few Americans left on the field were running low on ammunition. By 4:00 p.m., the American army was in complete disarray and wisely retired toward Cornwall, which had been taken from the British by General Jacob Brown earlier that day. The Battle of Crysler's Farm was over, a testimony to the value of British training and tactics. Morrison's small army suffered heavily, with 22 men killed and 148 wounded, but the American casualties were heavier, at 102 killed, 237 wounded, and over 100 captured.

Wilkinson was in Cornwall on November 12 when he learned of Hampton's loss at Chateauguay and of his decision to go into winter quarters. Wilkinson followed suit, taking his army across the St. Lawrence and going into winter quarters at French Mills, on the Salmon River in New York, just south of Cornwall. The 1813 campaign against Montreal was over, and that city would not again be threatened during the war. In the forest at Chateauguay and the wheat fields of John Crysler's farm, fewer than 1,500 British regulars, Canadian regulars, Canadian militia, and Native warriors had driven back 12,000 of the enemy and saved Montreal.

The End of the 1813 Campaign

News of American failures in the battles of Chateauguay and Crysler's Farm encouraged the British to again advance toward Niagara in force. However, they arrived too late. On December 10, 1813, American General McClure at Fort George, holding the fort with a rapidly shrinking garrison, most of whom were poorly trained and ill, decided to abandon the American bridgehead at Niagara. The American army marched out of Fort George and burned the town of Niagara and then retreated to the American side of the Niagara River.

The British arrived to find the town in ruins and the inhabitants facing the rigours of a very severe winter. They hastily found shelter for the civilians and planned a daring attack on the Americans at Fort Niagara. On December 19, they crossed the Niagara River and attacked the fort, capturing it at bayonet point. For the rest of the war, the Niagara frontier would remain in British hands. At the end of 1813, the American armies had failed to capture Kingston or Montreal and could not hold the Niagara frontier. A small American army held Amherstburg, the only Canadian territory still occupied by their troops. The new year would start off with more promise for a conquest of Upper Canada.

6

Hearts of Oak: The War at Sea

When the United States declared war on Great Britain on June 18, 1812, the forces of the fledgling Navy of the United States, as it was then known, constituted a diminutive David compared to the Goliath of Britain's Royal Navy. At the time of the declaration of war, the United States had 17 ocean-going vessels, the largest being three frigates rated to carry 44 guns each. The Royal Navy had 862 vessels at sea, some of which carried over 100 guns. The Halifax to West Indies station was patrolled by 79 vessels, including three large ships of over 74 guns, 23 frigates, and 53 smaller vessels, sloops, brigs, and schooners. In terms of sheer numbers, Britain clearly had the upper hand. In spite of this, the American navy was to prove a real thorn in the British side, winning victories which greatly exceeded even the wildest expectations. The war on the Atlantic was a series of brilliant naval actions as the British tried unsuccessfully to blockade American ports. The war also provided golden opportunities for Canadian and American privateers, commercial craft which verged on piracy as they attacked

Schooners, reminiscent of those involved in the war, still occasionally ply the waters of the Great Lakes.

and captured enemy merchant ships, making the owners of the privateers rich.

The Royal Navy

As an island nation, Britain depended on a powerful navy to protect its trade routes and defend its possessions worldwide. In the long struggle with the French during the Napoleonic Wars, the Royal Navy was used to blockade enemy ports to keep the French fleet bottled up in port, and was able to land British military forces at any spot along the long enemy coastlines. Enemy colonies could be attacked at will by the powerful British fleets.

In 1805, Admiral Lord Horatio Nelson's fleet saved England from being overwhelmed by a French invasion. In that year, Napoleon had amassed a huge army and constructed and gathered together an assortment of barges and landing craft with which to launch an amphibious invasion of England. His army was far larger than the British army,

Naval Dockyard, Point Frederick, July 1815, *by Emeric Essex Vidal.*

by the British and others in the invincibility of the Royal Navy. Thus, at the outbreak of the War of 1812, the British had nothing but contempt for the small American navy and felt confident that any meeting between ships of the two countries would result in an easy victory for the Royal Navy. On June 10, 1812, eight days before the outbreak of war, the London newspaper, the *Statesman*, declared that "America certainly cannot pretend to wage war with us; she has no navy to do it with." While some Americans shared this sentiment, the officers of the American navy would prove this view false.

which could be overwhelmed by the French army once it was ashore in England. Before he could invade, however, he would have to neutralize the Royal Navy, which would wreak havoc on his flotilla if it was able to interfere with the cross-channel move. The French and Spanish combined forces to create a powerful fleet that would be used to protect the flotilla, but this fleet was discovered off Cape Trafalgar, on the Iberian Peninsula, by Nelson. In a daring attack on the French and Spanish, Nelson won the crucial Battle of Trafalgar, losing his life during the action but destroying or capturing enough of the enemy to ensure that the invasion could not take place.

The Royal Navy had its faults. Atrocious living conditions aboard ship and poor pay for sailors resulted in recruiting difficulties and forced the navy to rely on forced service or "impressment" to ensure that the ships could be manned. This led to poor morale. Ships' officers who were not skilled at training and managing crews efficiently could end up in command of a ship that was ineffective as a fighting machine. Some progressive captains, however, through good people-management skills, could create a "happy ship" whose crew worked the sails and guns with great speed and precision, transforming the ship into a powerful force.

The Battle of Trafalgar, along with other earlier Nelson victories at Copenhagen and Aboukir Bay in North Africa, had given Nelson super-hero status and had led to the belief

The Navy of the United States

The American navy was small but fiercely proud and very professional. Building on the experiences of Revolutionary War heroes like John Paul Jones, the United States filled its navy with well-trained, bright young officers, and relied on strong, heavily armed, and very fast frigates. Frigates were two-deck ships with clean lines, known for their ability to outfight anything of similar size and to outsail anything larger.

American sailors volunteered for the service, and although they lived under the same crowded on-board conditions as their British counterparts, their ships docked in ports more frequently and the sailors were given shore leave when possible. The Royal Navy feared that sailors given shore leave, particularly those who had been "pressed" into the service, would take the opportunity to desert. The Americans, by contrast,

A British seaman, *by J.C.H. Forster.*

trusted their volunteers to return to the ship when required. A surprising number of Royal Navy deserters found their way into the American navy, where their experience was valued and promotion was fast.

Many of the American officers had campaign experience fighting the Barbary corsairs in the Mediterranean in 1801, and most had been guests of Royal Navy officers aboard British ships during peacetime. Their brief campaign experiences hardened them to the chaos of battle. In addition, their familiarity with the Royal Navy made the flaws of the senior service evident. When the war broke out, the officers and men of the Navy of the United States knew that they were more than a match for the Royal Navy, provided that they were to meet His Majesty's ships in ship-to-ship combat in which their numbers were equally matched.

American Victories at Sea

Three days after the declaration of war, American Commodore John Rodgers sailed off Sandy Hook, New Jersey, with a squadron consisting of his flagship frigate *President* (44 guns), the frigates *United States* (44 guns) and *Congress* (36 guns), the sloop *Hornet* (18 guns) and the brig *Argus* (16 guns). He had information that a British convoy of 100 merchant ships was sailing for England from Jamaica, and he was planning to intercept and capture or destroy as many of these ships as possible. The *President* spotted a sail on the horizon while cruising off New York and gave chase, soon pulling ahead of the other ships of the squadron.

The ship being chased by the *President* was not one of the Jamaica convoy, but the British frigate *Belvidera* (36 guns), commanded by Captain Richard Byron, who saw that the American frigate was larger than his ship and was also accompanied by other ships. He set a course for Halifax to

Armaments mounted on the ramparts of Halifax Citadel.

escape the American squadron. The *President* slowly gained on the *Belvidera* and, when finally within range, less than 2,000 metres behind the British ship, Commodore Rodgers ordered a couple of "bow chasers," the only guns on the ship which could fire forward, to open fire. These first three shots, the first shots fired in the War of 1812, hit the British ship, killing and wounding nine British sailors, the first casualties of the war. The guns were reloaded and fired again, but one of the guns burst, causing another powder charge being carried to the gun to explode. This explosion of just under four kilograms of powder in the confined space of the enclosed gun deck killed and wounded 16 Americans, including Commodore Rodgers, who was standing on the deck above. He was thrown into the air and broke his leg on landing but, refusing medical aid, he continued to command the action.

The *Belvidera* returned fire with its "stern chasers," guns which could fire from the rear of the ship at targets behind it. For the next two days, the action continued, with the *Belvidera* desperately trying to escape the *President*, and both ships firing when in range, to try to bring down rigging and thereby cripple the enemy ship. To lighten its load and thereby slightly increase speed, the *Belvedira* cut loose the ship's boats towed behind, discarded its heavy anchors, and finally pumped the barrels of fresh drinking water out of the hold and into the sea. Gradually it pulled out of range of the American ship and arrived at Halifax on June 26 with a report on the aggressiveness and impressive sailing abilities of the Americans.

A disappointed Commodore Rodgers sailed back to find his outpaced squadron, rejoining them a few days later. On July 1, sailing off the Grand Banks, Rodgers noticed a slick of fruit rinds, coconut shells, and other flotsam, indicating the passage of the elusive Jamaica fleet. He followed the trail for days, and by July 13 was only a few hundred kilometres from the coast of England. He turned back toward home, finally reaching Boston on August 29. On the way home he was able to capture eight small merchant ships as prizes. This helped to enrich the crew but still left Rodgers itching to match his ship against one of the Royal Navy.

On July 16, American Captain Isaac Hull in his 44-gun frigate *Constitution* was cruising off the New Jersey coast when his lookout reported five ships on the horizon. Hull mistook these for the five ships of Rodgers' squadron returning from their patrol. Hull sailed forward, hoisting signal lanterns into the shrouds displaying the American recognition signals. Too late he realized his mistake. The five ships were the Royal Navy ship *Africa* (64 guns), the frigates *Shannon* (38 guns) and *Guerriere* (38 guns), the *Aeolus* (32 guns), and the *Belvidera* which had returned from Halifax and which had captured the United States brig *Nautilus* (14 guns) the day before. This British squadron was under the command of one of the best Royal Navy officers, Captain Phillip Bowes Vere Broke. To make matters worse for Hull, the wind started to die at that point and without the wind, a sailing ship was helpless.

What happened next became an American naval legend and testimony to the toughness of the American sailors. Hull launched his ship's boats and ran tow lines to the heavy, cumbersome *Constitution*. Relays of sweating sailors and officers manned the boats to try to tow the ship out of danger. Hull pumped out as much drinking water as possible and threw anything considered expendable overboard. Little headway was made although the ship was moved some distance, but soon the British launched their own boats to attempt the same manoeuvre. Hull then had all of the rest of the spare ropes aboard the *Constitution* spliced together to make one exceedingly long rope. This was attached to a kedging anchor which would be rowed out ahead of the ship and dropped into the sea. The other end of the rope was then attached to the capstan (a type of winch) aboard the ship and sailors proceeded to winch the ship slowly toward the anchor. The procedure was then repeated. Meanwhile, the boats continued

A painting depicting the battle between the Constitution *and the* Guerriere, *by Thomas Birch.*

to try and tow the ship. The British followed the American example but undoubtedly the American sailors, facing the prospect of being overwhelmed by the British squadron, were more motivated to work a little harder. The *Constitution* was slowly pulling away. After three days and nights of this back-breaking labour, a light breeze began to shiver the sails. Pumps wet the sails down to catch any breath of wind, and finally the *Constitution* was able to escape after the breeze turned into a light squall. A course was set for Boston to reprovision and give the exhausted crew a rest.

The *Constitution* was at sea again in mid-August. At the same time, Broke detached the *Guerriere* from the British squadron to head back to Halifax to replenish its provisions. On August 19, a few hundred kilometres east of Halifax, the *Guerriere* caught sight of the *Constitution*, which was on the same course as the British ship. Although the *Constitution* (rated at 44 guns) was larger than the *Guerriere* (38 guns), Royal Navy Captain Dacres was confident that he could easily capture the American ship and take it into Halifax as a prize. He backed his sails, slowing the *Guerriere* to let the *Constitution* catch up. By 5:30 p.m., the ships were within range and the *Guerriere* opened fire. When they were only 50 metres apart, the *Guerriere* fired full broadsides at the

American ship, but many shots bounced off of its oaken sides. The *Constitution*'s guns remained ominously silent. When only 25 metres apart, Captain Hull finally gave the order, "now, boys, pour it into them!" The two ships stood side by side as the men worked like demons, firing, reloading, hoisting the heavy guns back up to their gunports, and firing again. The Americans were better trained, firing two shots for each one fired by the British.

Within minutes, the rigging of the *Guerriere* was tattered, and the masts knocked down, rendering the ship completely unmanageable. The *Constitution* drew off and the smoke slowly cleared. The *Guerriere* was a shambles, lying silently in the water with blood pouring from its scuppers but an ensign still bravely fluttering from the stump of the mizzenmast. The *Constitution* prepared to fire again, but the ensign was taken down from the *Guerriere* as the American ship approached. This "striking of the colours" was the normal signal for surrender, but Hull wanted to make sure. He sent a small boarding party by boat, and the American lieutenant in charge of the boarders was taken to Captain Dacres, where he asked the British captain if he had "struck." Captain Dacres reportedly replied "well, I don't know; our mizzen mast is gone, our main mast is gone, and, upon the whole, you may say we have struck our flag."

The *Guerriere* had paid a fearsome price for underestimating the seamanship and gunnery of the Americans. The ship was so battered that it could not be salvaged, and Hull was forced to set it on fire rather than attempt to tow it to an American port. The human cost was high with a third of the 300-man crew of the *Guerriere* killed or wounded. The *Constitution* had only seven men killed, and seven wounded. The ship had been built with green oak, which still retained its flexibility. Many of the British shots bounced off, giving rise to the ship's nickname, "Old Ironsides." The *Constitution* survives to this day, the oldest commissioned ship in the United States Navy.

The defeat of the *Guerriere* shocked the men of the Royal Navy, the people of Halifax, and the British people when the news got out concerning the battle. The idea of an upstart Yankee ship beating one of the proud vessels of the Royal Navy seemed unbelievable to those raised on the idea of its superiority. People tended to regard this as an anomaly. Surely the next time the two sides met the outcome would be different.

On October 8, Commodore Rodgers was again at sea with his squadron of three frigates and two smaller ships, again on the prowl for a British convoy. He soon detached the 44-gun *United States* under Captain Stephen Decatur and the 16-gun brig *Argus* to widen the search. In turn, Decatur detached the *Argus* to sail alone. Meanwhile, the British ship *Macedonian* (49 guns) under Captain John Carden had sailed from Portsmouth, England, bound for the West Indies. The ships met on the morning of October 25, opening fire at each other while still 2,500 metres apart. Again, the Americans outshot their British foe, firing twice as quickly as the men of the Royal Navy. Within 90 minutes, the *Macedonian* had its top masts shot away and had suffered more than 100 casualties. At noon, it surrendered to the *United States*. The captured British ship was patched up and escorted to New London, Connecticut, reaching port in early December. When news of the capture of a second British ship reached England, it was discounted as an unfounded rumour. No one believed that such a thing could happen twice.

On December 29, the *Constitution* was again in action, defeating the 46-gun Royal Navy frigate *Java* after a very bloody fight in which the British suffered 124 casualties while 58 men on the American ship were killed or wounded.

By the end of 1812, while the American army blundered about in the land battles in Upper Canada, the American navy had defeated three heavy frigates and three smaller British craft while losing only three small ships to Royal Navy vessels. The British finally woke up to the fact that the American navy was small but very professional. Admiral Sir John Warren, in Halifax, was sent reinforcements and soon had 15 huge 74-gun ships, a 50-gun ship, 15 frigates, and 20 sloops and brigs at his disposal. He was able to set up a blockade of American ports and to ensure that British ships never sailed alone.

Still, American ships continued to slip out of port to attack British merchant ships. One American frigate, the *Essex*, sailed around Cape Horn to cruise the Pacific. Until eventually cornered and captured by a British force, the *Essex* was able to capture or destroy numerous British whalers, primarily near the Galapagos Islands.

The spring of 1813 saw several actions between larger ships and smaller craft but no equal-sided battles occurred. American frigates would slip out of harbour to pounce on British sloops or schooners that were careless when reconnoitering American ports, while British ships remained ready to run down any American gun-boats or small ships patrolling the coast.

The *Shannon* and the *Chesapeake*

In late May 1813, the American 38-gun frigate *Chesapeake*, under Captain Lawrence, had just completed a refit and reprovisioning at Boston. Cruising out at sea and maintaining the blockade was the British frigate *Shannon* (38 guns) under Captain Broke, the officer who had chased the *Constitution* back to Boston in July 1812. Broke was one of the better officers of the Royal Navy. He worked his crew hard, practising their gunnery skills daily and insisting on excellence in sail and battle drill. His fair treatment of his men and his obvious abilities resulted in very high morale and professionalism aboard the *Shannon*. Lawrence, on the other hand, was still training many of the replacement crew for the *Chesapeake*, which had its share of newly recruited sailors. Broke challenged Lawrence to a sea duel and Lawrence, very aware of past American victories against British frigates, gladly accepted.

At 1:00 p.m. on June 1, as the old song goes, "the *Chesapeake* so bold, out of Boston we are told, came to take the British frigate neat and handy-o; while the people of the port all came out to see the sport and their band was playing Yankee Doodle Dandy-o." At 5:50, the *Chesapeake* came within range and the battle began. The skilled maneuvering of both captains made the battle akin to a dance of giants, with the large ships gracefully sliding through the water, each captain trying to position his ship to the greatest advantage, in order to bring its broadside guns to bear on the other ship's bow or stern, where few guns were located. Broke's crew outsailed the Americans and were able to fire the *Shannon*'s guns rapidly and accurately. Within a few minutes, the *Chesapeake* had been heavily damaged, and many of her crew were down, including Captain Lawrence, who was mortally wounded, shouting out "Don't give up the ship," a phrase that became a battle-cry in the United States Navy.

At 6:02, the two ships ground together. Broke yelled for volunteers to follow and jumped across to the deck of the American ship with his sword swinging. A fierce fight took place on the deck of the *Chesapeake* and although Broke was knocked down with a very serious head wound, he continued to encourage his men who soon overwhelmed the American sailors. At 6:05, a mere fifteen minutes after the ships had begun firing, the *Chesapeake* struck her colours. The *Shannon* had suffered 83 casualties while 146 men on the *Chesapeake* had been killed or wounded.

Several days later the people of Halifax were treated to the

H.M.S. *Shannon* towing American frigate *Chesapeake* into Halifax Harbour, 1813, *by J.C. Schetky.*

Lake Ontario Patrol 1814, by Peter Rindlisbacher.

most successful. On September 10, 1813, in the Battle of Lake Erie, American Commodore Oliver Hazzard Perry defeated and captured the entire British Lake Erie squadron.

The final year of war saw a continuation of the British blockade and no more major battles with the large American frigates. The main naval story was the use of the British fleet to land soldiers on American soil to try to capture American ports. A British raid on Washington, during which the Presidential mansion was burned along with other government buildings, achieved little. Fort McHenry in Baltimore was unsuccessfully bombarded by British ships for more than a day, but in the end the fort's flag still flew.

A British amphibious campaign on Lake Champlain in 1814 resulted in an American victory and British withdrawal. In the Battle of Plattsburg, well-handled American gunboats defeated a British flotilla and forced Prevost to call off his invasion of American territory.

In 1814, small ships fought a brutal war against each other with successes on both sides, but these actions had little impact on national morale and little effect on the war effort. More serious for both sides throughout the conflict was the amateur war being waged by the merchant mariners of Atlantic Canada and the coastal states.

site of the proud *Shannon* escorting the captured *Chesapeake* into harbour. The British losses of the previous year were avenged, and Broke was hailed as a hero. Church bells rang across Canada. When news of the capture reached London, the cannon of the Tower were fired in salute, a rare honour. Broke, crippled by his wound, was honoured for years in his home country. Lawrence died on his way to Halifax and was returned to the United States with great dignity. He also was respected as a hero by the British and Canadians of Halifax.

For the rest of 1813, the British retained the upper hand on the ocean, blockading all American ports, letting only a few American ships slip out, normally during bad weather when it was more difficult to keep station close to port. During the year, the American navy was able to capture only three small British vessels while the Royal Navy took the *Chesapeake* and two smaller craft. The American navy was still able to attack commercial shipping, however, capturing 79 British merchant vessels that year.

On Lake Ontario, the evenly matched fleets were at a stalemate as each side, Chauncey at Sackets Harbour and Yeo at Kingston built ever larger ships, upsetting and then restoring the balance of power and giving neither side an advantage. On Lake Erie, however, the Americans proved

The Privateers

Throughout history, commercial ships had been licenced to prey on enemy shipping during times of war, to augment the efforts of the navy and to disrupt enemy commerce. Official papers known as "letters of marque" proved that a ship was a duly licenced privateer rather than just an opportunistic pirate.

During the War of 1812, the United States government issued over 500 letters of marque to vessels of all sizes, from small coastal schooners bearing tiny crews and a small cannon to much larger ocean going vessels which carried as many guns and crew as some warships. American privateers cruised from South America to the North Sea, from the coast of Europe to the Gulf of St. Lawrence, pouncing on British merchant ships, fishing boats, and whalers, capturing about 1,300 British merchant vessels during the three years of war. This was not only a major blow to the British economy, but by the rules of privateering, the owner and crew of a successful ship could make a fortune from the sale of the captured ship and cargo.

Mahone Bay, Nova Scotia, where the Teazer's *captain destroyed his ship rather than have it captured by the British.*

The British rules regarding privateers and letters of marque were much more strict than those of the Americans, and at the outbreak of the war they issued only a few commissions to Canadian privateers, 49 such letters being given at Halifax and Saint John. Canadian privateers were required to land their booty at Halifax, Liverpool, or Saint John, where the sale of the goods and captured ships was strictly regulated. Still, the profits made from privateering by Canadian ships were enormous. During the war, over 200 American "prizes" were brought into Halifax, Saint John, Liverpool, Digby, and Yarmouth. More American merchants suffered at the hands of the Royal Navy, which was blockading American ports and was able to run down American ships trying to sneak out of or into port.

Many of these actions were dramatic. The American privateer *Young Teazer* was a major thorn in the side of the British maritime community. A sleek and powerful schooner, equipped with sails and long oars or "sweeps" for use in calm airs, the *Teazer* captured dozens of British merchant vessels. The ships of the Royal Navy kept a sharp lookout to try to destroy this menace, and the chance finally came on June 27, 1813, when it was sighted off Halifax. A British squadron chased the *Teazer* but lost it in a fog only to sight it again off Lunenburg. It was headed off by the large 74-gun ship *La Hogue* but the *Teazer*'s captain steered into Mahone Bay, which was too shallow for heavy navy vessels. However, the American schooner was trapped in the bay. The Royal Navy loaded men

in ships' boats to attack. When capture seemed inevitable, one of the *Teazer*'s officers went below and set fire to the ship's gunpowder magazine. The explosion caused the disintegration of the schooner, killing all but eight of the 38-man crew. Today, the chancel cross in the Anglican Church in Chester, Nova Scotia, is one of the few reminders of that day. The cross was made from a piece of timber from the *Young Teazer*.

The *Liverpool Packet*

During the war, while Halifax was the chief naval base in Canada, Liverpool was the chief port for Canadian privateers. Investors would build or purchase ships, outfitting them with guns as privateers, and hiring captains and crews to sail them. Captured enemy vessels and their cargoes, known as "prizes," would be sold through a "prize court" and make the owners, captains, and crews into wealthy men. The most successful Canadian privateer was the *Liverpool Packet*. Under Captain Joseph Barss, the *Liverpool Packet* gained many prizes early in the war. Barss knew the American coast well and understood that American coastal craft as well as ships returning from ocean voyages would use the tip of Cape Cod as a major navigation point, a spot that was the first landfall for ships sailing back to the United States and a major obstacle around which coastal vessels had to manoeuvre. Barss would lie in wait to bear down on and capture anything weaker than the *Packet*

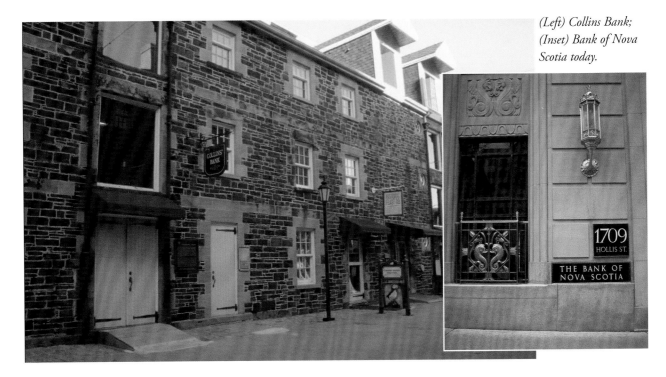

(Left) Collins Bank; (Inset) Bank of Nova Scotia today.

or, with his veteran crew and fast ship, make a hasty retreat when threatened by a larger ship. Under Captain Barss, the *Liverpool Packet* captured some 50 prizes from the Americans. The privateer was later commanded by Captain Caleb Seeley of Saint John, and under this able captain was able to snap up another 40 American boats.

Enos Collins of Nova Scotia was a major backer of privateers, including the *Liverpool Packet*, and made a fortune from his share of the "prize money" from captured ships and goods. By the war's end, he was considered to be the wealthiest man in North America. Collins used his fortune to establish several businesses, including the Halifax Banking Company, which later became the Bank of Nova Scotia. Thus, a modern Canadian institution can trace its ancestry back to the daring privateersmen of the War of 1812.

Economic Effects of the Naval War

The capture of British merchant vessels significantly affected shipowners and insurers during the war, and millions of dollars in ships and merchandise were lost. The war effort suffered to some extent, particularly when transport ships carrying military supplies or troops were captured by American naval or privateer vessels. The horses for the 17th Light Dragoons were captured, forcing that elite regiment to ride hired Canadian horses during the 1814 campaign on the Niagara frontier. Muskets desperately needed by the Canadian militia ended up in American hands, and the new red coats ordered by the 104th Regiment of Foot ended up on the backs of U.S. Army musicians. By and large, however, the naval war did not have a major impact on the British war effort. The Royal Navy and merchant fleets were just too large for the American navy to tackle, and for every British merchant ship captured, a hundred got through with their cargoes.

The war had a much more serious effect on American commerce, as the blockade stifled American trade. Manufactured goods, normally imported from Europe, became scarce and prices soared. American raw goods could not be shipped and rotted in waterfront warehouses. Fortunes were lost, and it is no surprise that many New Englanders remained thoroughly opposed to the war and breathed a sigh of relief when it ended on December 24, 1814.

7

The Final Invasions: The Summer of 1814

By the spring of 1814, the prospects for the American war effort were not encouraging for the army of the United States. Canada had been able to hold out against American invasions in 1812 and 1813. The confidence with which American soldiers marched in the early days of the war had been destroyed by more defeats than victories in a variety of battles and skirmishes. The early American successes on the Atlantic

Soldiers' barracks at Fort Erie.

Ocean were in the past, and now a much more powerful Royal Navy fleet kept the ports of the United States closed to all but the most daring skipper who could sneak past the blockading ships during dark nights or stormy days.

For the British, faced with a titanic struggle against Napoleon in 1812 when the United States had declared war, things were now looking up. The French armies had been forced to retreat from Moscow in 1812, and the British under the Duke of Wellington were finally driving the French out of the Iberian Peninsula by 1813. Final victory in Europe came and Napoleon was forced to abdicate on April 11, 1814. He would return to power to meet his final defeat at Waterloo on June 18, 1815, but

in the spring of 1814, he seemed to be utterly defeated. This had a great impact on the final year of the War of 1812.

George Prevost, the British commander-in-chief in North America, had adopted a defensive strategy in the first two years of the war. His main plan was to hold on to British strongpoints in the Canadas, particularly Montreal and Quebec, to do nothing that would risk large numbers of his small regular army defensive force, and to await reinforcements from Britain. The turn of the tide in the Peninsular War, with the French retreating from Spain, gave the British the confidence to send more troops to North America. By 1814, Prevost commanded almost 16,000 regulars and Canadian soldiers who had been trained to the same high standards as their British counterparts. His armies would soon be reinforced by an additional 10,000 regulars from Britain. Further, supplies of weapons, ammunition, uniforms, and other stores for issue to the Canadian militia had been arriving by convoys of transport ships.

By contrast, the American army was still in disarray. While the regular army theoretically had 23,000 men, almost

A memorial plaque at Burlington Heights.

half of these had enlistment terms that were ending early in 1814. There were thousands more militia in the United States, but these soldiers were untrained men led by ineffective officers. On the positive side, the regular army was becoming increasingly more professional. Under progressive young officers like Winfield Scott, some of the regiments had been trained to the high standards of their red-coated enemy. Americans had learned that to use the musket of the day most effectively, soldiers had to be well disciplined and willing to stand in close ranks and fire levelled volleys on command. The battles of 1812 and 1813, when American armies had been driven off by much smaller British and Canadian forces, were in the past, and the lessons of the value of well-ordered linear tactics had been learned.

The Americans and British in North America knew that the balance in Canada would be upset once the French were defeated in Europe. The Americans had come to the realization that they could not win the war, but still felt that they could gain major concessions in the inevitable peace treaty if they could make major inroads into Canada in 1814, thus giving themselves a stronger bargaining position at the diplomatic table. They knew that large numbers of British reinforcements would eventually arrive, so 1814 represented a last chance at gaining something from the war.

The 1814 American strategy was not markedly different from their failed plans of 1813. They still held the Detroit frontier and controlled southwestern Ontario. They now planned to recapture Niagara, proceed on to capture Burlington Heights (Hamilton), and push on to Kingston. Montreal would be threatened in order to prevent reinforcements from being sent to Upper Canada and, it was hoped, by the end of the campaign, the Americans would be in command of the lands west of Montreal.

In February 1814, U.S. Major-General Wilkinson moved his dwindling army from winter quarters at French Creek (Fort Covington) to Plattsburg, on Lake Champlain. His new plan was to move early into Lower Canada, capture the British post on Isle aux Noix in the Richelieu River, and use that strategic spot as a base for further operations against Montreal or the communications route of the St. Lawrence. His army set off in mid-March, capturing the Canadian border town of Odelltown en route to Isle aux Noix. On March 30, his 4,000-man army arrived at Lacolle Mill, a fortified post guarding the crossing of the Lacolle River, the last obstacle before reaching a spot opposite Isle aux Noix. Defending the mill was a small force of 200 British and Canadians, who stalled the Americans while 800 British reinforcements raced from Isle aux Noix. The British were now almost 1,000 strong and included a troop of Royal Marine Artillerymen armed with a terrifying new weapon, the Congreve rocket. These new weapons were exploding shells propelled by rockets mounted on long poles, which rushed through the air, spitting sparks and making an unearthly moan in flight. The rockets caused few casualties but, combined by heavy musket fire from the defenders of Lacolle Mill, proved too much for Wilkinson's army. The Americans retreated to Plattsburg. Shortly after this event, Wilkinson left the area to return to Washington, where he was forced to defend his conduct of the campaign the previous autumn to avoid the indignity of a court martial.

This brief campaign represented the last American threat to Montreal. In September 1814, Prevost was powerful enough to finally take the offensive, threatening to drive the Americans out of Plattsburg and off of Lake Champlain, but he was no more successful than the American generals had been in their attempts on Montreal. The second phase of the campaign on the Niagara frontier would be a much greater threat to the British.

The Battle of Chippawa

In the early summer of 1814, the British maintained garrisons and outposts along the Niagara River, from Fort Erie to Fort George. Fort Niagara in New York State had been captured by the British the previous December, and along with the new British Fort Mississauga on the opposite Canadian shore, the British firmly controlled the mouth of the Niagara River. The Niagara frontier was commanded by

Major-General Phineas Riall, who had about 1,700 regulars under his command. He could also call on several hundred well-trained Canadian militia and a few hundred Native allies if threatened.

The American army opposing the British was about 4,000 strong, a quarter of which were New York and Pennsylvania militia. The commanding officer, Jacob Brown, now a major-general, had two very professional assistants, the previously mentioned Brigadier-General Winfield Scott, who had been promoted since the 1813 campaign, and Brigadier-General Eleazar Ripley. These men had trained the regulars to a very high level of proficiency during the winter and spring. The American army also included a number of professional artilleryman and 100 equally well-trained cavalrymen. He had also enlisted the assistance of 400 Six Nations warriors, primarily Senecas from the New York side of the Niagara River. Through April and May, Scott drilled the troops relentlessly and ensured that all had been issued with new uniforms. Blue cloth was in short supply so the army had sent grey jackets for Brown's troops along with regulation blue. Scott dressed one regiment in blue but put the rest of the men in the new grey uniforms, ensuring that for the coming campaign, most of his regulars were issued the same colour of coat.

Finally, all was ready and orders were given for the troops to leave Buffalo and cross the Niagara River to invade Canada once again. On the early morning of July 3, the first invasion boats under Winfield Scott grounded on the Canadian beach near Fort Erie, where the invaders came under heavy British musket fire. As more Americans landed, the British defenders fell back to the protection of the fort. General Brown arrived with the bulk of the forces by dawn and set his force in motion to attack Fort Erie, which was manned by only 137 British soldiers. As the Americans positioned a heavy cannon to fire

Village of Chippawa, by George Heriot. On July 4, 1814, American general Winfield Scott began his advance toward the Chippawa River with 1,300 men.

on the fort, the British officer in command of the post asked for a "parley," to discuss terms for a possible capitulation. After much negotiation but no further fighting, Fort Erie surrendered in the late afternoon. Brown's army had captured Fort Erie at little cost and now had a firm foothold on Canadian soil. Brown sent scouts ahead to reconnoitre the land toward Niagara and ordered his troops to encamp near Fort Erie. In the meantime, British General Riall, at Fort George, had learned from his cavalrymen of the American invasion.

On July 4, Brown ordered Winfield Scott to advance to the Chippawa River with his brigade of 1,300 men with artillery support and a squad of cavalry dragoons. Setting off from camp about noon, Scott continually fought skirmishes against an elite unit of British soldiers under Lieutenant-Colonel Thomas Pearson, who defended each creek along the American route of advance, stopping Scott's force with a few musket and cannon shots and then retiring to the next creek along the line of march. By late afternoon, Scott's force had reached Street's Creek, several hundred yards from the

Battle of Chippawa. *The British harassed Scott's force all the way to Chippawa, stopping for a skirmish at every creek along the way.*

harass the Americans and reconnoitre their position to estimate their strength and numbers. His scouts caused a few casualties in the American camp and reported that the Americans were primarily militiamen, dressed in grey, the uniform normally associated with militia. In fact, this was Scott's brigade of highly trained regulars. The idea that the enemy were similar in number to his own forces and the belief that they were militia led Riall to plan a bold attack which, based on past experience, would surely rout the supposedly untrained militia manning Street's farm. He started his forces across the Chippawa River at about noon. This manoeuvre would take some time, but was concealed from the Americans by a stand of trees between Street's Creek and the Chippawa River.

Chippawa River, where the British maintained a palisaded blockhouse. Scott marched his men toward the Chippawa River, but was fired on by British cannon on the other side. This stopped Scott's brigade, which now set up camp to await the arrival of the rest of the American army. Around midnight, Brown arrived at Street's Creek with more troops, bringing the American force to 2,000 men.

At Chippawa, British General Riall had arrived with additional forces. He now had 1,400 regulars, 200 local militiamen from the 2nd Lincoln Regiment, 70 cavalrymen of the 19th Light Dragoons, and militia cavalrymen from Niagara's Provincial Light Dragoons. Also with Riall were 300 Native allies from the Six Nations and from the western tribes who had fought for Tecumseh the previous year. Riall also had about 70 artillerymen manning two large 24-pounder field guns, three more mobile 6-pounders, and a 5-inch howitzer that could fire exploding shells.

Early the next morning, the American camp came under sniper fire from the woods west of Street's fields. Riall had sent part of his militia force with the Native warriors to

Meanwhile, Brown decided to do something about the bothersome gunfire of the Canadians and Natives from the woods on his flank. Brigadier-General Peter Porter had arrived in camp with 200 militiamen and about 300 Seneca warriors who had allied themselves to the American cause. At about 3:00 p.m., Brown ordered Porter's force and a small backup company of 56 regulars to "scour the woods" and drive off the Canadians.

A vicious see-saw battle took place in the woods, where the men of both forces moved in the dense underbrush, firing at each other from a few metres distance and filling the woods with dense powder smoke. The Canadian force was pushed back but was reinforced, forcing Porter's Native allies to retreat. As Porter's militia and regulars entered the fray, they in turn pushed the Canadians back toward Chippawa. By this time, most of Riall's army had crossed the river, and he sent his well-trained light infantry troops to help against Porter's forces. The calm and well-ordered volleys of musket fire by these troops proved the deciding factor, and the

American force finally retreated toward their camp.

The volume of musket fire from the woods, and particularly the regular volleys by the British light infantry, made Brown realize that this was more than a mere skirmish. He ordered Winfield Scott to form his brigade on Street's field, just as Riall's force emerged from the woods from the direction of Chippawa and took position at the far end of the field. The British artillery opened fire on the Americans, who now rushed to place their own cannon in position. The Americans had twice the number of artillery pieces, and a regular artillery duel began. Under heavy fire, Scott's troops marched in perfect order across Street's Creek to take position in a long line facing the British, with the river on their right and the woods, still full of skirmishers, on their left. When the British saw how calmly and professionally the Americans marched under fire, they recognized that they were not militia, but well-disciplined troops. Legend says that Riall, watching the Americans take position, said "Why! These are Regulars."

Riall now realized that the Americans would not be as easy to defeat as he had thought but he was still confident. Based on the performance of American regulars in the past, he was sure that his troops were more than a match for an American army of the same size, whether or not they marched well. He deployed his forces, with the 1st or Royal Scots Regiment and the 100th Regiment ranged in a line facing the American line, and the 8th or King's Regiment slightly back on the right flank, close to the woods to counter the American 25th Regiment deployed on that side. It was just after 4:00 p.m.

With regimental flags flapping in the breeze, company drummers beating the cadence, and bayonets flashing in the late afternoon sun, the red-coated lines made an intimidating sight as they slowly marched toward the American line, keeping their ranks straight and orderly, shoulder to shoulder in two ranks or rows. The American artillery fired at the advancing force, but gaps in the front ranks were quickly filled by those behind to keep a solid front facing the enemy. When the British were within musket range, the American line fired a volley. As the smoke cleared, the British line could be seen still slowly approaching, then halting, straightening their line and preparing to fire. For the next 15 minutes, the two forces exchanged volleys at close range. Riall had ordered his line so that only the men of the 100th and 1st Regiments could take clear shots at the Americans, and his artillery could not fire from their position at the American infantry for fear of hitting the British infantry. The Americans were much better deployed, with an army that was a little larger and which was gradually being reinforced. Their line was longer than the British line, which allowed some of their troops to fire into the flanks of the British. Also, their artillery was better sited to fire on the British troops without having to fire over the heads of their own men.

Riall could see the heavy casualties being inflicted on his men and knew that the musketry duel could not continue. A bayonet charge was ordered, but the men would not advance against the solid American line. They had expected a quick

Those are Regulars! *was Riall's cry when he discovered the grey-coated Americans were not militia. Painting by H.C. McBarron.*

The Chippawa battlefield today looks much as it would have in 1814.

States Army by 1861, claimed that the cadets of the West Point Military Academy wore their famous "cadet grey" uniforms in honour of his grey-clad division at the Battle of Chippawa.

Lundy's Lane

Within a couple of days of the Battle of Chippawa, the American army was able to cross the Chippawa River upstream of the British position. Riall ordered the British fortifications at the village of Chippawa abandoned, and marched his men back to Fort George and to a position near present-day St. Catharines. Brown followed with the American army, advancing to Queenston Heights to prepare for a final assault on the British in southern Ontario. He could scan Lake Ontario from Queenston and was waiting for Commodore Chauncey to arrive off the Niagara River with the American fleet. Together, he thought, they would take the new Fort Mississauga and recapture Fort George and Fort Niagara. They would then advance on Burlington Heights before a final assault on Kingston. But these plans could not be carried out.

At this time, Chauncey's American fleet did not have control on Lake Ontario. Chauncey's fear was that if he took the fleet to Niagara, Commodore Yeo would attack from Kingston and capture the American naval base of Sackets Harbour. Chauncey's fleet remained protecting Sackets Harbour or reconnoitering Kingston to keep an eye on Yeo's fleet. Chauncey himself remained ill throughout this period and stayed at his base. Brown did not know this and kept his main army at Queenston while sending small groups of men out to scour the countryside for supplies and to scout for any British movement. Skirmishes with patrols of British regulars, Canadian militia, or Native warriors were frequent, and the Americans burned a number of farms where skirmishes took place in retaliation for the attacks on American soldiers. On July 18, an American troop was involved in a sharp fight in

victory over poorly trained troops, but instead met trained regulars who were their match in professionalism. Casualties had been heavy, particularly among the officers. Riall reluctantly had his bugles blow the signal to retire. His men shouldered their muskets and in an orderly fashion marched back away from the Americans, leaving a carpet of their dead and severely wounded on the field. The British recrossed the Chippawa River and destroyed the centre section of the bridge to prevent an American pursuit.

The Battle of Chippawa was over. The British, Canadian, and Native force had lost over 100 men killed and three times that number had been wounded while 58 Americans had been killed and 318 wounded. More importantly, for the first time in their country's history, an American army had won a battle against a force of roughly equal size. Prior to this, American armies had only been victorious when they vastly outnumbered the enemy. It was a proud moment that marked the beginnings of a well-trained professional United States Army. Winfield Scott, who continued his military career, becoming the top ranking general in the United the village of St. Davids, a few kilometres from Queenston. The British were driven off and the American officer had his men burn the entire village. Brown was infuriated by this act and dismissed this officer from the American army.

Brown decided to advance toward Lake Ontario, expecting to see Chauncey's fleet at any time. The Americans surrounded Fort George and Fort Mississauga, which fired cannon at them, but the range was too distant for much damage to be done. The Americans began to set up cannon batteries to fire on Fort George, but when it became clear that Chauncey's fleet would not arrive, everything was loaded back onto wagons and Brown's army withdrew to Queenston on July 22. Two days later, they marched further back to Chippawa to reorganize. There was now a plan to march directly to Burlington, effectively cutting Niagara off from supplies and reinforcements.

As the Americans left, Major-General Riall ordered his army to advance cautiously toward Queenston in order to keep watch on Brown's army. Lieutenant-Colonel Thomas Pearson took 1,000 regulars for the task, reaching Queenston and then continuing along the Portage Road into the area which is now the city of Niagara Falls. His force finally arrived at Lundy's Lane, a major crossroads, and took up a position on a high point of land surrounded by clearings. Riall followed with a second force to back him up. During this time, the British had been rushing troops to the Niagara front, regiments having set out on the road from Kingston, York, and Burlington, all converging on Niagara to finally drive the American army from Canadian soil.

Lieutenant-General Gordon Drummond, commander-in-chief of Upper Canada, arrived at Fort George with more troops. He ordered a detachment of the 1st, 8th, and 41st regiments, accompanied by a force of Native warriors, to advance from Fort Niagara on the American side of the river to capture American cannon which had been threatening Fort George, and to continue on to capture Lewiston Heights opposite Queenston. He ordered Lieutenant-Colonel Morrison's 89th Regiment, the heroes of the Battle of Crysler's Farm, to catch up with Riall's force, which was marching to reinforce Lieutenant-Colonel Pearson at Lundy's Lane.

In the American camp, Major-General Brown learned of the British advance on Lewiston and feared that his sup-

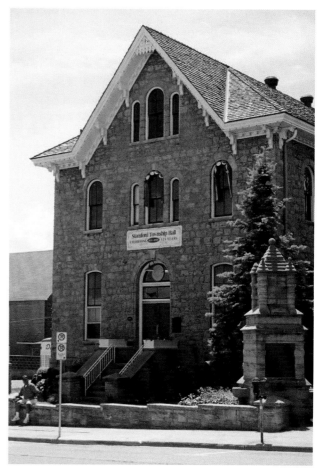

The Lundy's Lane Museum in Niagara Falls.

plies at Fort Schlosser, just upriver from Niagara Falls, would be threatened by this force. He ordered Brigadier-General Winfield Scott to advance toward Queenston along the Portage Road to delay the British advance on the Canadian side of the river and to assess the situation. In the meantime, the British force at Lewiston recrossed the Niagara to Queenston, and the regulars in this group marched to join their comrades at Lundy's Lane while the bulk of the Native forces returned to Fort Niagara and Fort George. There were now 1,000 British at Lundy's Lane, with another 800 reinforcements under Lieutenant-Colonel Morrison approaching that spot, while an additional 1,200 men who had been brought by Colonel Hercule Scott from Burlington Heights, were not far behind, heading for the position at Lundy's Lane.

In the late afternoon, Winfield Scott's American brigade of 1,100 men neared Lundy's Lane. On seeing this column, General Riall at the British position assumed that Brown's entire American army was approaching, and began to withdraw pending the arrival of more British troops. Soon, however, General Drummond arrived with the first contingent of British reinforcements and repositioned his force of 1,600 men along the roadway. His artillery was positioned among the tombstones of a cemetery that covered the top of the highest point of land above Lundy's Lane, overlooking the Portage Road along which the Americans were advancing, parallel with the River.

At about 7:15, as shadows were lengthening, Winfield Scott started his assault on the British position by ordering his men into line across the fields and marching toward the British position, only to halt a few hundred yards downhill from their defences, out of effective musket range. He was reluctant to attack uphill, and hoped to entice the British to attack his force. The British infantrymen stayed put while the Royal Artillerymen opened up on the Americans with two heavy 24-pounder guns, two 6-pounders, and the 5-inch howitzer that had been used earlier in the month at Chippawa. With the British force was a troop of rocketeers of the Royal Marine Artillery, who fired the terrifying but ineffective Congreve rockets toward the American troops. Casualties mounted, and while smaller American squads fought brisk firefights with the British at closer range from woods on the flanks, the main American force stood their ground while their soldiers continued to be killed and wounded by the British artillery fire.

At about 9:00, just after sunset, the American brigades, under Generals Ripley and Porter, arrived to reinforce Scott's decimated army. Under cover of the dark night, the Americans advanced on several fronts and succeeded in over-

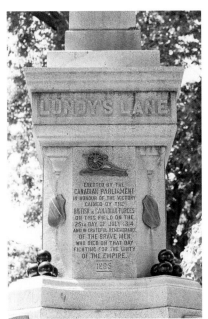

Lundy's Lane monument on Drummond Hill.

running the hill, driving back the British and capturing the British artillery. At this time, British Colonel Hercule Scott arrived with his reinforcement of about 1,200 men and the British and Canadians re-formed to attack the Americans and retake the cannon.

Three times in the next few hours the British charged the American positions, only to be driven back by gunfire. The battlefield was confusing, the flashes of artillery and musketry providing the only light on a dark night that was thick with the fog of gunpowder smoke. Men fired at each other from distances as short as one metre, some fired on their own troops, mistaking them for the enemy, and many were captured by the enemy as they blundered into enemy-held positions, mistaking foe for friend. The scene would have been terrifying, filled with the crash of musket volleys, the staccato popping of rifles, the thunder of cannon, the cries and moans of wounded men, and the pitiful sounds from the wounded horses of the artillery.

After the Americans had driven off the third British charge, the redcoats regrouped for yet another assault, pausing to replenish ammunition supplies and to quench their thirst with swigs from their canteens. Many of the men were exhausted, having marched since daybreak. During this lull, the Americans assumed that the British would not return. They were low on ammunition, out of drinking water, and had hundreds of wounded men on their hands, including many of their officers, among whom were Generals Scott and Brown. They decided to retire to Chippawa to rest and regroup before planning their next move. The British were therefore able to reoccupy the hill without a fight.

The next morning, the sun unveiled the scene of horror which lay on the small field of battle. Over 250 bodies were sprawled in the grass, among the graves on the hill, and in groups where cannon had scythed through their ranks. Dead horses littered the area where the British

Grave at Drummond Hill. Hull was killed in the Battle of Lundy's Lane.

artillery had been stationed. Each side had brought almost 3,000 men to the battle. On the American side, 173 men had been killed and 571 wounded, while the British counted 84 dead and 559 wounded. Both sides had lost over 100 men as prisoners. The British survivors tended the wounded and gathered the dead, burying the British and some of the Americans in shallow trenches. The exhaustion of the men and the increasing heat of the day made the task of finding graves for all of the corpses too daunting. Finally, three pyres were built with fence rails, and the majority of American dead were cremated.

Both sides claimed to have won the Battle of Lundy's Lane, based on who occupied the hill at the end of the day. Generations of historians have continued the argument. While different criteria for victory will suggest different conceptions of the "winner," the fact remains that the American force suffered so heavily and the British force at Niagara proved so large, that the Americans realized that there was no hope in pursuing the objectives of the 1814 campaign. They could not take Niagara, let alone Burlington and Kingston. The American army withdrew to Fort Erie and greatly strengthened the fortifications while Drummond brought the bulk of his army back to Queenston.

The Siege of Fort Erie

Once the British looked after their casualties and replenished their food and ammunition supplies, they were ready to renew their attack on the American army, now entrenched in an armed camp centred on Fort Erie. On July 30, Drummond set out from Queenston and began the march to Fort Erie, arriving there in a few days. A detachment was sent across the Niagara to attack American supply bases at Black Rock and Buffalo, but they were driven back by

American riflemen. The American army at Fort Erie, which now stood at about 2,100 effectives, had strongly fortified the former British fort. Major-General Brown was still recovering from his wounds in Buffalo, but ordered his army to hold Fort Erie as a bridgehead for possible future actions against Upper Canada.

Drummond decided on a proper attack on Fort Erie, breaking down the defences with cannon fire before launching an assault. A few days were spent building cannon batteries and defensive positions. This process was delayed by cannon fire from three American schooners anchored near the fort. In a night-boat action, two of these vessels were captured by British sailors and soldiers on August 12. The following day, the British cannon batteries opened fire on the defences of Fort Erie, with the plan to create a breach that could be exploited by an infantry assault. In fact, the gun emplacements were firing at long range and did little damage to the fort. Nonetheless, on August 14, Drummond readied his men for a night assault.

The poorly planned and executed night assault on Fort Erie in the early hours of August 15 resulted in vicious fighting at the American defences, soldiers fighting with bayonets and their bare hands. At one of the bastions, the British were able to overwhelm the Americans after scaling the earthworks with ladders. The American cannon were turned by the British soldiers in order to fire on the rest of the fort, but a spark ignited the powder magazine in the bastion and caused a devastating explosion just before dawn. The blast killed or wounded hundreds of the redcoats, and the assault quickly ended with the British returning to their siege lines. During the night assault, Drummond's army had suffered over 900 casualties, at least 222 men having been killed. This assault had proven more deadly than the Battle of Lundy's Lane.

For the next few weeks it rained daily. Although the troops continued to fire at each other, and small skirmishes occurred each day, more men were laid low by sickness than by enemy action. While the siege of Fort Erie dragged on, the British army in other parts of North America was on the move. The war against Napoleon was over, and reinforcements were sent to gain victories which could be used for leverage as peace talks continued at Ghent, Belgium, between the Americans and British. In late August, Royal Navy ships carried an army

Fort Erie.

to the heart of America. On August 24, following the Battle of Bladensburg, Maryland, a victorious British army marched to Washington and drove off the defenders, burning the government buildings of the capital. This created a legend. The scorched presidential mansion was whitewashed to hide the stains and is still known as the White House. On September 13, a British amphibious force attempted to capture American Fort McHenry but the fort stood through a relentless bombardment and the British failed to force the garrison to surrender. This event's most enduring legacy was the penning of the "Star Spangled Banner" by a witness.

In early September, General Prevost, at the head of an army of 10,000 men, could now abandon the defensive posture which he had taken since the outbreak of the war. He led his men down Lake Champlain, planning to capture the American base at Plattsburg before proceeding further inland. His naval escort was defeated at the Battle of Plattsburg, however, and Prevost retreated back to Montreal with his troops.

Back at Fort Erie, the Americans received reinforcements on September 9 and 10. The wet weather, the advancing season, the fear of an American assault on Fort George, and the realization that a heavy price would be paid if Fort Erie was to be taken, made the British decide to lift the siege. While they were preparing to leave, the Americans surprised them by launching a full-scale sortie from the fort on the morning of September 17. Casualties were very heavy on both sides,

with over 500 Americans and 600 British, Canadians, and Natives killed, wounded, or missing. The Americans returned to Fort Erie, and the British were able to continue to break up their encampment, leaving the area on September 21 and heading back to Niagara.

Small American forces continued to use Fort Erie as a base for raids against British outposts, clashing with them at Chippawa on October 15 and at Cook's Mill a few days later, but the war was winding down in this region as winter approached.

The Americans decided that it was too hazardous to try to hold Fort Erie through the winter and on November 5 they abandoned the fort, blew up its defences, and withdrew from Canadian soil. They went into winter quarters at Buffalo to plan the 1815 campaign, during which, they hoped, an invasion of Upper Canada would finally meet with success. They never had to act on their plans.

On Christmas Eve, 1814, the American and British delegates who had been meeting in Belgium signed the Treaty of Ghent to end the War of 1812. Captured territory, including the British-held Fort Niagara and the American-held Fort Malden in Amherstburg, were to be returned to their original owners. There were no territorial gains as a result of the war. Thousands of lives had been lost, the villages of Niagara, St. Davids, Youngstown, and Lewiston, had been destroyed, and many civilians in the war zones had suffered incredibly. Americans did gain something in that Britain would now carefully respect American sovereignty on the high seas and in the western frontier lands that Americans would occupy, dispossessing the Native people who lived there.

As at the beginning of the war, news travelled slowly. The bloodiest battle of the war was fought at New Orleans on January 8, 1815, two weeks after the Treaty of Ghent was signed. News of the treaty reached President Madison in Washington a month later, and it was ratified on Valentine's Day. Sporadic skirmishes occurred for the next two months as news slowly spread to the furthest outposts. By spring, the last action had been fought.

Conclusion

The War of 1812 has been called "the war that both sides won" and "the war that no one won." It has left us with a legacy, a strong sense of the importance of defending what we hold dear. For the people who lived in the war zones in which the battles were fought, the conflict was a total war. It saw Canadians of all backgrounds banding together to work with the British army to drive off the American invaders. It built a sense of deep pride in Canada, but it also ultimately led to the idea that such a war between neighbours should never happen again. Although there were threats of renewed war with the Americans in 1838, 1866, and 1870, the United States of America and Canada have now become close allies and good friends. It is a relationship which was forged in the fire of the War of 1812, and consecrated by the blood of the men and women who were casualties of the conflict.

A Hundred Years of Peace, by Amedee Forestier, depicts the signing of the Treaty of Ghent, ending the war. (Inset) Six Nations veterans of the War of 1812.

Historical Documents

War Declared, June 18, 1812

British: Colonel Baynes to Major-General Brock, Quebec, June 25, 1812

"Sir, — Sir George Prevost desires me to inform you that he has this instant received intelligence from Mr. Richardson by an express to the Northwest Company, announcing that the American Government had declared war against Great Britain. This dispatch left New York on the 20th instant, and does not furnish any other circumstance of intelligence whatever."

American: Governor Tompkins to Hon. Wm. Eustis, Secretary at War, Albany, June 27, 1812

"Sir, — Your letter of the 19th inst., announcing the important intelligence of a declaration of war against the United Kingdom of Great Britain and Ireland and its dependencies, was received on Tuesday evening at eleven o'clock."

Capture of Detroit, August 16, 1812

British: Major-General Brock to Major Thomas Evans, Detroit, August 17, 1812

"Dear Evans, — Detroit is ours, and with it the whole Michigan Territory, the American army prisoners of war. The force you so skilfully prepared and forwarded at so much risk met me at Point au Pins in high spirits and most effective state. Your thought of clothing the militia in the 41st cast off clothing proved a most happy one, it having more than doubled our own regular force in the enemy's eye."

American: Army General Orders, Lewiston, August 28, 1812

"The army under the command of Brigadier-General Hull has surrendered at Detroit. This is a national disaster, but it is the duty of soldiers to turn even disasters to profit. To this end the General calls upon the troops under his command to make every effort in perfecting that discipline on which they must rely for their own safety and for their country's honor in that crisis which may be fast approaching."

Battle of Queenston Heights, October 13, 1812

British: Major-General Roger Hale Sheaffe to Sir George Prevost, Fort George, October 13, 1812

"Sir, — I have the honor of informing Your Excellency that the enemy made an attack with considerable force this morning before daylight on the position of Queenston. On receiving intelligence of it Major-General Brock immediately proceeded to that post, and I am excessively grieved in having to add that he fell whilst gallantly cheering his troops to an exertion for maintaining it. With him the position was lost, but the enemy was not allowed to retain it long, reinforcements having been sent up from this post, composed of regular troops, militia, and Indians. A movement was made to turn his left, while some artillery, under the able direction of Captain Holcroft, supported by a body of infantry, engaged his attention in front. This operation was aided, too, by the judicious position which Norton and the Indians with him had taken on the woody brow of the high ground above Queenston. A communication being thus opened with Chippawa, a junction was formed with succours that had been ordered from that post. The enemy was completely defeated. I had the satisfaction of receiving the sword of their commander, Brigadier General Wadsworth, on the field of battle, and many officers, with upwards of 900 men were made prisoners, and more may yet be expected. A stand of colors and a 6-pounder were also taken. The action did not terminate till nearly three o'clock in the afternoon, and their loss in killed and wounded must have been considerable. Ours I believe to have been comparatively small in numbers. No officer was killed besides Major-General Brock, one of the most gallant and zealous officers in His Majesty's service, whose loss cannot be too much deplored, and Lieut.-Colonel Macdonnell, Provincial aide-de-camp, whose gallantry and merit render him worthy of his chief."

American: Major-General Stephen Van Rensselaer to Hon. Wm. Eustis, Secretary of War, Lewiston, October 14, 1812

"Colonel Van Rensellaer with great presence of mind ordered his officers to proceed with rapidity and storm the fort [the redan battery on Queenston Heights]. This service was gallantly performed and the enemy driven down the hill in every direction. Soon after this both parties were considerably reinforced, and the conflict was renewed in various places. Many of the enemy took shelter behind a stone guard-house, where a piece of artillery was now briskly served. I ordered the fire of our battery to be directed upon the guard-house, and it was so effectually done that with eight or ten shot the fire was silenced. The enemy then retreated behind a large stone house, but in a short time the rout became general and the enemy's fire was silenced except by a one-gun battery so far down the river as to be out of the reach of our heavy ordnance, and our light guns could not silence it. A number of boats now passed over unannoyed, except by the one unsilenced gun. For some time after I had passed over the victory seemed complete, but in expectation of further attacks I was taking measures for fortifying my camp immediately.

But very soon the enemy were reinforced by a detachment of several hundred Indians from Chippawa. They commenced a furious attack, but were promptly met and routed by the rifle and bayonet. By this time I perceived my troops were embarking very slowly. I passed immediately over to accelerate their movements, but to my utter astonishment I found that at that very moment when complete victory was in our hands the ardor of the unengaged troops had entirely subsided. I rode in all directions; urged the men by every consideration to pass over, but in vain.

At this time a large reinforcement from Fort George was discovered coming up the river. The reinforcements...formed a junction with the Indians in the rear of the heights. At this critical moment I despatched a note to General Wadsworth, acquainting him with our situation, leaving the course to be pursued much to his own judgement, with the assurance that if he thought best to retreat I would endeavour to send as many boats as I could command, and cover his retreat by every fire I could safely make. But the boats were dispersed; many of the boatmen had fled panic-struck, and but few got off. The enemy succeeded in repossessing the battery and gaining advantage on every side. The brave men who had gained the victory, being exhausted of strength and ammunition, and grieved at the unpardonable neglect of their fellow soldiers, gave up the conflict.

I can only add that the victory was really won, but lost for the want of a small reinforcement; one-third of the idle men might have saved all."

Frenchtown or the River Raisin, January 22, 1813

British: Gentleman Volunteer John Richardson to Charles Askin, Amhertsburg, February 4, 1813

"You have doubtless heard ere this of the engagement at the River Raisin on Friday, the 22nd inst. (ult.); however, you may probably not have heard the particulars of the business, which are simply these: On Monday, the 18th, we received information that the Americans, under the command of General Winchester, after an obstinate resistance, had driven from the River Raisin a detachment of Militia under Major

Reynolds (also a party of Indians) which had been stationed there some time. That they had sustained great loss from the fire of our Indians, and from a 3-pounder, which was most ably served by Bombardier Kitson (since dead), of the R.A.

On Tuesday part of our men moved over the river to Brownstown, consisting of a Detachment of R. Artillery, with 3 3-pounders and 3 small howitzers, Capt. Tallon's Company (41st Regt.), a few Militia, and the sailors attached to the Guns. An alarm was given that the enemy were at hand. The Guns were unlimbered and everything prepared for action, when the alarm was found to be false. On Wednesday the remainder of the army joined us at Brownstown, where (including Regulars, Militia, Artillery, Sailors and Indians) we mustered near 1,000 men. We lay, this night, at Brownstown. Next day the army commenced its march towards the River Raisin and encamped, this night, at Rocky River, which (you know) is about 12 miles beyond Brownstown and 6 on this side the River Raisin. About two hours before day we resumed our march. On Friday at daybreak we perceived the enemy's fires very distinctly — all silent in their camp. The army drew up and formed the line of battle in 2 adjoining fields, and moved down towards the enemy, the Guns advanced 20 or 30 paces in front and the Indians on our flanks. We had got tolerably near their Camp when we heard their Reveille drum beat (so completely lulled into security were they that they had not the most distant idea of an enemy being near), and soon after we heard a shot or two from the Centinels, who had by this time discovered us. Their Camp was immediately in motion. The Guns began to play away upon them at a fine rate, keeping up a constant fire. The Americans drew up and formed behind a thick picketing, from whence they kept up a most galling fire upon our men, who, from the darkness of the morning, supposed the pickets to be the Americans; however, as it grew lighter, they discovered their mistake, and advanced within 70 or 80 paces of the pickets, but finding that scarce one of their shots took effect, as they almost all lodged in the fence. Being thus protected from the fire of our men they took a cool and deliberate aim at our Troops, who fell very fast, and the most of the men at the Guns being either killed or wounded, it was thought expedient to retire towards the enemy's left under cover of some houses. I was a witness of a most bar-barous act of inhumanity on the part of the Americans, who fired upon our poor wounded, helpless soldiers, who were endeavouring to crawl away on their hands and feet from the scene of action, and were thus tumbled over like so many hogs. However, the deaths of those brave men were avenged by the slaughter of 300 of the flower of Winchester's army, which had been ordered to turn our flanks, but who, having divided into two parties, were met, driven back, pursued, tomahawked and scalped by our Indians, (very few escaping) to carry the news of their defeat. The General himself was taken prisoner by the Indians, with his son, aide, and several other officers. He immediately dispatched a messenger to Colonel Procter, desiring him to acquaint him with the circumstance of his being a prisoner, and to intimate that if the Colonel would send an officer to his Camp to summons the remainder of his army to surrender, he would send an order by him to his officer then commanding to surrender the Troops. Colonel Procter objected to sending one of his own officers, but permitted the General to send his aide (with a flag). The firing instantly ceased on both sides, and about 2 hours afterwards the enemy (460 in number) laid down their arms and surrendered themselves prisoners of war. A good many of our officers were wounded in the engagement, but none of them killed. The following is a list of them: R.A., Lt. Troughton (slightly); Seamen attached to the Guns, Capt. Rolette, Lt. Irvine, Midshipman Richardson (severely); 41st Regt., Capt. Tallon, Lieut. Clemow (severely); Militia, Inspecting F. Officer Lt.-Col. St. George, Capt. Mills, Lt. McCormick, Paymaster Gordon (severely); Ensign Gouin (slightly); R. N. F. Regt, Ensign Kerr (dangerously); Indian Depart., Capt. Caldwell, Mr. Wilson (severely). This is as accurate an account as I can give you of the Engagement. I will now give you an account of my feelings on the occasion. When we first drew up in the field I was ready to fall down with fatigue from marching and carrying a heavy musket. Even when the balls were flying about my ears as thick as hail I felt quite drowsy and sleepy, and, indeed, I was altogether in a very disagreeable dilemma. The night before at Rocky River, some one or other of the men took my firelock and left his own in the place. It being quite dark when we set out from that place, I could not distinguish one from another. Enquiry was vain, so I was obliged to take the other (without thinking that anything was the matter with it). When we came to the firing part of the business I could not get my gun off. It flashed in the pan, and I procured a wire and worked away at it with that. I tried it again, and again it flashed. I never was so vexed — to think that I was exposed to the torrent of fire from the enemy without having the power to return a single shot quite disconcerted the economy of my pericranium; though if I had fired fifty rounds not one of them would have had any effect, except upon the pickets, which I was not at all ambitious of assailing like another Don Quixote. Our men had fired 4 or 5 rounds when I was called to assist my brother Robert, who was wounded, and who fell immediately, and which led me to suppose that he was mortally wounded. However, when he was carried to the doctors I found the poor fellow had escaped with a broken leg, which torments him very much, and it will be some time before he gets over it. I think it is highly probable we shall have a brush with the valiant Harrison, who is said to be at the Rapids of the Miami River, or near them. If so, I think we shall have tight work, as we have lost in killed and wounded in the action of the 22nd 180 men (exclusive of Indians). Pray remember me to my cousins."

American: Augustus Porter to Peter B. Porter, Buffalo, February 3, 1813

"Sir, — Before you receive this you will undoubtedly have heard of he defeat and capture of General Winchester's division of Harrison's army. As to the truth of the report, it yet remains all uncertainty as to particulars, tho' I have no doubt a battle has been fought and a number of our men have been taken, but so great a part of the army yet remains as very much disturbs the people on the Canada side, as on yesterday and today all the force of the enemy from the river have moved westward, it is supposed with a view to meet the main body of the N.W. army. I presume there is not now on the whole river 300 men left, and yet the famous army of the Centre makes not a single movement to produce a diversion in favour of the N.W.A. [north west army of the United States], but are snugly hutted at the Eleven Mile Creek, and fearing that the military stores on the lines may be disturbed are moving them to their camp for protection, and leave the

defenceless inhabitants to protect themselves. What are the Government about? Why do they not send some man here to command who will do something and not let our armies be cut up in detail."

Capture of Ogdensburg, February 22, 1813

British: Major George Macdonnell of the Glengarry Light Infantry, Lieutenant-Colonel Commanding in the Eastern District of Upper Canada, to Colonel Baynes, Prescott, February 22, 1813

"Sir — I have the honour to acquaint you for the information of His Excellency, the Commander of the Forces, that in consequence of His Excellency's commands to retaliate, under favourable circumstances, upon the enemy for his late wanton aggression on this frontier, I, this morning about seven o'clock, crossed the river St. Lawrence upon the ice and carried, after a little more than an hour's action, his position in and near the opposite town of Ogdensburg, taking eleven pieces of cannon and all his ordnance, marine, commissariat and quartermaster general's stores, 4 officers and 70 prisoners, and burning two armed schooners and two large gunboats and both barracks. My force consisted of about 480 regulars and militia and was divided into two columns. The right, commanded by Captain Jenkins of the Glengarry Light Infantry Fencibles, was composed of his own flank company and about 70 militia, and, from the state of the ice and the enemy's position in the old French fort, was directed to check his left and interrupt his retreat whilst I moved on with the left column, consisting of 120 of the King's Regiment, 40 of the Royal Newfoundland corps, and about 200 militia, towards his position in the town, where he had posted his heavy field artillery. The depth of the snow in some degree retarded the advance of both columns and exposed them, particularly the right, to a heavy cross fire from the batteries of the enemy for a longer time than I had expected, but pushing on rapidly after the batteries began to open upon us the left column soon gained the right bank of the river, under the direct fire of his artillery and line of musketry posted on an eminence near the shore. Moving on rapidly, my advance, consisting of the Royal Newfoundland

and some select militia, I turned his right with the detachment of the King's Regiment, and after a few discharges from his artillery took them with the bayonet and drove his infantry through the town, some escaping across the Black River into the fort, but the majority fled to the woods or sought refuge in the houses, from whence they kept such a galling fire that it was necessary to dislodge them with our field pieces, which now came up the bank of the river, where they had stuck on landing in the deep snow....

The enemy had 500 men under arms and must have sustained a considerable loss.

Return of Killed and Wounded in the Action
    Royal Artillery — One private killed.
    8th or King's Regiment — One sergeant killed, two privates wounded.
    Glengarry Light Infantry — Two privates killed; Lieut.-Colonel Macdonnell, Capt. Jenkins, Lieut. McKay, two sergeants and seven rank and file wounded.
    Militia — Two rank and file killed; Captain J. Macdonnell, Lieuts. Empy, McLean and McDermott, one sergeant and fifteen rank and file wounded."

American: Captain Benjamin Forsyth to Colonel Macomb, February 22, 1813

"Sir, — I have only time to inform you that the enemy, with a very superior force, succeeded in taking Ogdensburg this morning about nine o'clock. They had two men to our one, exclusive of Indians. Numbers of the enemy are dead on the field. Not more than twenty of our men killed and wounded. Lieutenant Beard is among the latter. I have made a saving retreat of about eight or nine miles. I could not get all the wounded off.

We have killed two of the enemy to one of ours killed by them. We want ammunition and some provisions sent on to us, also sleights for the wounded.

If you can send me three hundred men all shall be retaken and Prescott, too, or I will lose my life in the attempt. I shall write you more particularly today."

Capture of York, April 27, 1813

British: Sir Roger Hale Sheaffe to Sir George Prevost, Kingston, May 5, 1813

"Sir — I did myself the honour of writing to Your Excellency on my route from York, to communicate the mortifying intelligence that the enemy had obtained possession of that place on the 27th of April."

American: Major-General Dearborn to the Secretary of War, Headquarters, York, Capital of Upper Canada, April 27th, 1813, 8 o'clock p.m.

"Sir — We are in full possession of this place, after a sharp conflict in which we lost some brave officers and soldiers.

General Sheaffe commanded the British troops, militia and Indians, in person. We shall be prepared to sail for the next object of the expedition the first favourable wind."

American: Commodore Chauncey to the Secretary of the Navy, United States Ship Madison, *at anchor off York, 8 o'clock P.M., April 27, 1813*

"Sir — I have the satisfaction to inform you that the American flag is flying upon the fort at York. The town capitulated this afternoon at 4 o'clock."

Capture of Fort George, May 27th, 1813

British: Brigadier-General Vincent to Sir George Prevost, Forty Mile Creek, May 28, 1813

"Sir — I have the honor to inform your Excellency that yesterday morning about daybreak the enemy again opened [fire from] his batteries upon Fort George. The fire not being immediately returned, it ceased for some time. About 4 o'clock a.m. a combination of circumstances led to to a belief that an invasion was meditated. The morning being exceedingly hazy neither his means nor his intention could be ascertained until the mist, clearing away at intervals, the enemy's fleet, consisting of 14 or 15 vessels, was discovered under way standing towards the lighthouse in an extended line of more than two miles, covering from 90 to 100 large boats and scows, each containing an average of 50 or 60 men. Though at this time no doubt could be entertained of the enemy's intention his points of attack could only be conjectured. Having again commenced a heavy fire from his fort, line of batteries and shipping, it became necessary to withdraw all the guards and piquets station along the coast between the fort and the lighthouse, and a landing was effected at the Two Mile Creek, about half a mile below the latter place. The party of troops and Indians stationed at this point, after opposing the enemy and annoying him as long as possible, were obliged to fall back, and the fire from the shipping so completely enfiladed and scoured the plains that it became impossible to approach the beach. As the day dawned the enemy's plan was clearly developed, and every effort to oppose his landing having failed, I lost no moment in concentrating my force and taking up a position between the town, Fort George and the enemy, there awaiting his approach....

Being on the spot and seeing that the force under my command was opposed with ten-fold numbers, who were rapidly advancing under cover of their shipping and batteries, from which our positions were immediately seen and exposed to a tremendous fire of shot and shells, I decided on retiring my little force....Having given orders for the fort to be evacuated, the guns to be spiked and the ammunition destroyed, the troops under my command were put in motion and marched across the country in a line parallel to the Niagara river, towards the position near the Beaver Dams...."

American: Major-General Dearborn to Governor Tompkins, Niagara, Fort George, Upper Canada, May 27, 1813

"Dear Sir,

We took possession of Fort George and its immediate dependencies this day. Our loss does not exceed thirty killed and forty-five wounded. We have ascertained that the enemy had upwards of seventy killed and above 150 wounded. We made upwards of 100 prisoners. We had only one officer killed, Lieut. Hobart, my grandson. We have much more to do. Our troops behaved like brave old soldiers."

The *Shannon* and the *Chesapeake*, June 1, 1813

British: Captain Philip Broke to Captain the Hon. T. Bladen, on board Shannon, *Halifax, June 6, 1813*

"Sir, — I have the honour to inform you, that being close in with Boston light-house in H.M.S. [His Majesty's Ship] under my command, on the 1st inst. I had the pleasure of seeing the US frigate *Chesapeake* (whom we had long been watching) was coming out of the harbour to engage the *Shannon*; I took a position between Cape Ann and Cape Cod and then hove-to for him to join us. The enemy came down in a very handsome manner, having three American ensigns flying; when closing with us he sent down his royal-yards. I kept *Shannon*'s up, expecting the breeze would die away.

At half past 5 PM the enemy hauled up within hail of us on the starboard side, and the battle began, both ships steering full under their topsails; after exchanging between two and three broadsides, the enemy's ship fell on board us, her mizen channels locking in with our fore rigging. I went forward to ascertain her position; and observing the enemy were flinching from their guns, I gave orders to prepare for boarding. Our gallant hands appointed to the service immediately rushed in, under their respective officers, upon the enemy's decks, driving everything before them with irresistible fury. The enemy made a desperate but disorderly resistance. The firing continued at all the gangways, and between the tops, but in two minutes time the enemy were driven sword in hand from every post. The American flag was hauled down and the proud British Union floated triumphant over it. In another minute they ceased firing from below and called for quarter. The whole of this service was achieved in 15 minutes from the commencement of the action."

American: Letter from Lieutenant George Budd, Navy of the United States, to the Secretary of the Navy Board, Halifax, June 15, 1813

"Sir, — The unfortunate death of captain James Lawrence, and lieutenant Augustus C. Ludlow, has rendered it my duty to inform you of the capture of the late United States frigate *Chesapeake*.

On Tuesday, June 1st, at 8 A.M. we unmoored ship, and at meridian got under way from President's Roads, with a light wind from the southward and westward, and proceeded on a cruise. A ship was then in sight in the offing, which had the appearance of a ship of war, and which, from information received from pilot-boats and craft, we believed to be the British frigate *Shannon*. We made sail in chase, and cleared the ship for action. At half past 4 P.M. she hove to with her head to the southward and eastward. At 5 P.M. took in the royals and top-gallant sails, and at half past 5, hauled the courses up. At 15 minutes before 6 P.M. the action commenced within pistol shot. The first broadside did great execution on both sides, damaged our rigging, killed among others, Mr White, the sailing master, and wounded captain Lawrence. In about 12 minutes after the commencement of the action, we fell on board of the enemy and immediately after, one of our arm chests on the quarter deck was blown up by a hand-grenade thrown from the enemy's ship. In a few minutes, one of the captain's aids came on the gun-deck to inform me that the boarders were called. I immediately called the boarders away, and proceeded to the spar deck where I found that the enemy had succeeded in boarding us, and gained possession of our quarter-deck. I immediately gave orders to haul on board the fore-tack, for the purpose of shooting the ship clear of the other, and then made an attempt to regain the quarter-deck but was wounded and was thrown down on the gun-deck. I again made an effort to collect the boarders, but in the mean time the enemy had gained complete possession of the ship. I there found captain Lawrence and lieutenant Ludlow, both mortally wounded; the former had been carried below, previously to the ship's being boarded; the latter was wounded in attempting to repel the boarders."

Battle of Stoney Creek, June 6, 1813

British: Army General Orders, Headquarters, Kingston, June 8, 1813

"His Excellency the Commander of the Forces has just received an express announcing that a strong division of the enemy had advanced to the Forty Mile Creek with the intention of attacking the position occupied by Brigadier-General Vincent at the head of Burlington Bay. The enemy's plan was, however, anticipated by the gallant General and completely defeated by a spirited attack at day-break on the 6th instant on the American army, which was completely defeated and dispersed."

American: Secretary of War to General Dearborn, War Department, June 19, 1813

"There is indeed some strange fatality attending our efforts. I cannot disguise from you the surprise occasioned by the two escapes of a beaten enemy; first on the 27th ultimo [capture of Niagara, May 27], and again on the 6th instant. Battles are not gained when an inferior and broken enemy is not destroyed."

Battle of Beaver Dams, June 24, 1813

British: Lieutenant-Colonel Bisshopp to Brigadier-General Vincent, June 24, 1813

"Sir — I have the honor to inform you that the troops you have done me the honor to place under my command have succeeded in taking prisoners a detachment of the United States Army under Lieut.-Colonel Boerstler.

In this affair the Indians under Captain Kerr were the only force actively engaged: to them great merit is due, and I feel particularly obliged for their gallant conduct on this occasion. On the appearance of the detachment of the 49th, under Lieutenant FitzGibbon, and the light company of the 8th or King's Regiment and the two flank companies of the 104th under Major De Haren, and the Provincial Cavalry under Captain Hall, the whole surrendered to His Majesty's troops. To the conduct of Lieut. FitzGibbon, through whose address the capitulation was entered into, may be attributed the surrender of the American troops."

American: Lieutenant-Colonel Charles G. Boerstler to Major-General Dearborn, June 25, 1813

"Sir — I am permitted to state the misfortune which has befallen myself and the detachment entrusted to my care.

We proceeded yesterday morning until near Beaver Dams when we were attacked by a large number of Indians, who were reinforced by regulars under Colonel DeHaren, while other reinforcements marched in the direction of our rear. The action lasted 3 hours, 10 minutes, during which time we drove them some distance into the wood, but finding our men not equal in that mode of fighting I changed my position twice during the engagement to get more open ground, but such was the situation that the enemy's [musket] balls reached us from every direction, while he was concealed. Our ammunition being nearly expended, surrounded on all sides, seventeen miles to retreat when my force would have constantly diminished while the enemy was gathering in from various outposts I saw that in the exhausted state the men were in that the far greater part could never reach Fort George (if any), therefore was compelled to capitulate."

Certificate written about Laura Secord by James FitzGibbon, Toronto, February 23, 1837

"I do hereby certify that Mrs. Secord, wife of James Secord of Chippawa, Esquire, did in the month of June, 1813, walk from her house in the village of St. Davids to DeCoo's house in Thorold, by a circuitous route of about twenty miles, partly through the woods, to acquaint me that the enemy intended to attempt by surprise to capture a detachment of the 49th Regiment, then under my command, she having obtained such knowledge from good authority, as the event proved."

Action at Butler's Farm, July 8, 1813

British: Colonel Claus to Lieut.-Colonel Harvey, Ten Mile Creek, July 9, 1813

"Sir, — I received your note of the 7th about 12 o'clock the same night, and I immediately went to the camp and collected a body of Indians [Six Nations and Ottawas with other western aboriginal men]. I gave the necessary directions to Capt. Norton [war-chief of the Six Nations]. At daylight 100 and odd left camp. About 4 p.m. information was received that they were engaged with the enemy. I collected the Indians that remained in camp and was just proceeding to join them when a party appeared with five prisoners. I found that after the defeat of the foregoing party near Mr. Ball's, on the Two Mile Creek, a reinforcement of about 1,000 men advanced as far as the piquet by Mr. Butler's and returned almost immediately, as appears by the enclosed Brigade Order No. 3. The riflemen, who were out for the purpose of covering the foregoing party, retired as soon as they perceived the Indians. From what I can collect the killed and prisoners amount to upwards of 100. Of the latter there are 12. Of ours none killed; two Indians and one interpreter wounded, the other very slightly in the hand."

American: Major B.M Malcom, 13th United States Infantry, to Mr. Samuel Eldridge, Camp near Fort George, July 18, 1813 (on the death of Lt. Eldridge)

"On the morning of the 8th inst. our advanced picket was attacked. I immediately volunteered to take command of a force sufficient to meet the enemy. Upon my having obtained this permission he (Lieut. Eldridge) nobly said; 'I must go along with you.' I directed him to join me at a certain point. After my departure a battle having commenced, he was determined to meet me by a nearer route than ordered, and in endeavouring to fall on the left of my detachment he was cut off by the enemy, who by this time had gained the ground over which he was to pass, and in endeavouring to force his way he fell, having lost 20 of his little command."

Battle of Lake Erie, September 10, 1813

British: Major-General Procter to Major-General De Rottenburg, September 12, 1813

"Sir, — With the deepest regret I acquaint you that the squadron of His Majesty's vessels, *Detroit, Queen Charlotte, Lady Prevost, Hunter, Erie,* two ships, schooner brig, small schooner, sloop, six sail, under the command of Captain Barclay, sailed at 3 o'clock p.m. on the 9th inst. to seek that of the enemy, nine sail, two brigs, carrying 20 32-pound carronades each and two long 12-pounders and that on the 10th inst. the two fleets were seen engaged between the islands, about 25 miles from the settlement below Amherstburg. The action lasted from twelve to nearly half-past three ..., and the firing was incessant .... The spectators were fully impressed with the idea that our fleet were the victors, but circumstances have since placed it beyond a doubt that the whole of our fleet has been taken or destroyed."

American: Commodore Olivery Hazard Perry to General William Henry Harrison, on board the Lawrence, *September 10, 1813, 4:00 p.m.*

"We have met the enemy and they are ours — Two Ships, two Brigs, one Schooner and one Sloop."

Battle of the Thames (Moraviantown), October 5, 1813

Shawnee: Speech by Tecumseh to Procter as the British prepared to abandon Amherstburg, September 18, 1813

"Father, listen! Our fleet has gone out; we know they have fought; we have heard the great guns; but we know nothing of what has happened to our father with one arm [British commodore Barclay]. Our ships have gone one way, and we are much astonished to see our father tying up every thing, to run the other way, without letting his red children know what his intentions are. You always told us to remain here and take care of our lands. You always told us you would never draw your foot off British ground; but now, father, we see you are drawing back, and we are sorry to see our father doing so without seeking the enemy. We must compare our father's conduct to fat dog that carries its tail upon its back, but when afrighted it drops it between its legs and runs off.

Father, listen! The Americans have not yet defeated us by land, neither are we sure that they have done so by water; we therefore wish to remain here and fight our enemy, should they make their appearance. If they defeat us we will then retreat with our father....You have the arms and ammunition which our great father, the king, sent for his red children. If you have an idea of going away, give them to us, and you may go and welcome for us. Our lives are in the hands of the Great Spirit. We are determined to defend our lands, and, if it be his will, we wish to leave our bones upon them."

Canadian: Thomas G. Ridout to Thomas Ridout, Burlington Heights, October 16, 1813

"We had a most dreadful time from the Cross Roads [the British army retreated from what is now Virgil in Niagara-on-the-Lake on hearing exaggerated rumours of Procter's defeat]. Upwards of 300 men were straggling upon the road, and waggons loaded with miserable objects stuck fast in mudholes, broken down and unable to ascend the hills, and the men too ill to stir hand or foot. One thousand Western Indians arrived last night from Detroit, besides 2,000 women and children. Poor creatures! What will become of them? It is said the great Tecumseh is killed. The Indians have made horrid work with Harrison's army, killing several hundred. We are sending all the heavy baggage to York but do not think Sir George will allow this army to retreat.

The troops have left the Forty. Vincent is waiting for orders from below before he retreats."

British: Major-General De Rottenburg to Sir George Prevost, October 16, 1813

"Sir, — Your Excellency will perceive from the enclosed copies of letters just received from Major-Generals Vincent and Procter that affairs in that quarter are by no means so disastrous as has been most shamefully represented by Staff Adjutant Reiffenstein, whose false reports and speculations upon the extent and consequences of Major-General Procter's defeat have been openly circulated by that officer and have created the greatest alarm throughout the whole country."

Battle of Chateauguay, October 26, 1813

British: General Orders, Headquarters, La Fourche on the Chateauguay River, October 27, 1813

"His Excellency the Governor-in-Chief and Commander of the Forces has received from Major-General De Watteville, the report of the affair which took place in front of the advanced positions of his post at 11:00 o'clock on Tuesday morning, between the American army, under the command of Major-General Hampton, and the advanced piquets of the British, thrown out for the purpose of covering working parties under the direction of Lieutenant-Colonel De Salaberry. The judicious position of his little band, composed of the Light Company Canadian Fencibles and two companies of Canadian Voltigeurs, repulsed with loss the advance of the enemy's principal column, commanded by General Hampton in person, and the American Light Brigade under Col. McCarty, was in like manner checked in its progress on the south side of the river by the gallant and spirited advance of the flank company 3rd Embodied Militia, under Captain Daly, supported by Captain Bruyer's Company of Sedentary Militia; Captains Daly and Bruyer being both wounded and their companies having sustained some loss, their position was immediately taken up by a flank company of the First Battalion Embodied Militia. The enemy rallied and repeatedly returned to the attack, which terminated only with the day in his complete disgrace and defeat, being foiled by a handful of men not amounting to a twentieth part of the force opposed to them ...."

American: Major-General Hampton to the Secretary of War, Head Quarters, Four Corners, November 1, 1813

"On advancing near the enemy, it was found that the column on the opposite side [of the river] was not so far advanced as had been anticipated. The guides had misled it and finally failed in finding the ford. We could not communicate with it but only waited the attack below. About two o'clock the firing commenced and our troops advanced rapidly to the attack. The enemy's light troops commenced a sharp fire, but Brigadier-General Izard advanced with his brigade, drove him everywhere behind his defences and silenced the fire in his front. This brigade would have pushed forward as far as courage, skill, and perseverance could have carried it, but on advancing it was found that firing had commenced on the opposite side and the ford had not been gained.

The enemy retired behind his defences, but a renewal of his attack was expected and the troops remained some time in their positions to meet it. The troops on the opposite side were excessively fatigued. The enterprise had failed in its main point, and Colonel Purdy was ordered to withdraw his column to a shoal four or five miles above and cross over [the

river]. The day was spent and General Izard was ordered to withdraw his brigade to a position three miles in the rear, to which place the baggage had been ordered forward.

It [was] necessary for the preservation of this army, and the fulfilment of the ostensible views of the Government, that we immediately return by orderly marches to such a position as will secure our communications with the United States, either to retire into winter quarters or be ready to strike below."

Battle of Crysler's Farm, November 11, 1813

British: Lieutenant-Colonel Joseph Wanton Morrison, 89th Regiment, to Major-General De Rottenburg, Christler's, Williamsburg, Upper Canada, November 12, 1813

"Sir, — I have the heartfelt gratification to report the brilliant and gallant conduct of the detachment from the Centre Division of the army as yesterday displayed in repulsing and defeating a division of the enemy's force, consisting of two brigades of infantry, and a regiment of cavalry, amounting to between 3,000 and 4,000 men, who moved forward about two o'clock in the afternoon from Christler's Point and attacked our advance, which gradually fell back to the position selected for the detachment to occupy, the right resting on the river and the left on a pine wood, exhibiting a front of about 700 yards.

The ground being open the troops were thus disposed, the flank companies of the 49th Regiment, the detachment of the Canadian Fencibles with one field piece, under Lieut.-Colonel Pearson on the right, a little advanced on the road; three companies of the 89th Regiment under Captain Barnes with a gun formed in echelon with the advance on its left supporting it. The 49th and 89th thrown more to the rear, with a gun, formed the main body, and the reserve extending to the woods on the left, which were occupied by the Voltigeurs under Major Heriot and the Indians under Lieut. Anderson. At about half-past two the action became general, when the enemy endeavored by moving forward a brigade from his right to turn our left, but was repulsed by the 89th forming en potence with the 49th and both corps moving forward, occasionally firing by platoons. His efforts were next directed against our right, and to repulse this movement the 49th took ground in that direction in echelon, followed by the 89th; when within half-musket shot the line was formed under a heavy but irregular fire from the enemy.

The enemy...concentrated their force to check our advance, but such was the steady countenance and well directed fire of the troops and artillery, that about half-past four they gave way at all points ...."

American: Brigadier-General John P. Boyd to Major-General Wilkinson, Camp near Cornwall, November 12, 1813

"Sir, — I have the honor to report to you that yesterday while the rear division of the army, consisting of detachments from the 1st, 3rd, and 4th Brigades and placed under my command to protect the flotilla from the enemy that hung on our rear, was under arms in order to move, agreeably to your orders, down the St. Lawrence, a report was brought to me from the rear-guard that a body of about two hundred British and Indians had advanced into the woods that skirted our rear. General Swartwout with the 4th Brigade was immediately ordered to dislodge them, General Covington with the 3rd Brigade being directed to be within supporting distance. General Swartwout dashed into the woods and with the 21st Infantry (a part of his brigade) after a short skirmish drove them back to the position of the main body. Here he was joined by General Covington. The enemy had judiciously chosen his ground among the deep ravines which everywhere intersected the extensive plain, and discharged a heavy and galing fire upon our advancing columns. No opposition or obstacle, however, checked their ardour. The enemy retired more than a mile before their resolute and repeated charges. During this time the detachment of the 1st Brigade under Colonel Coles, whose greater distance from the scene of action retarded its arrival, rapidly entered the field.

Being directed to attack the enemy's left flank, this movement was promptly and bravely executed amid a shower of musketry and shrapnel shells. The fight now became more stationary until the brigade first engaged, having expended all their ammunition, were directed to retire to a more defensible position to wait for a re-supply. This movement so disconnected the line as to render it expedient for the 1st Brigade

likewise to retire .... When the artillery was finally directed to retire, having to cross a deep and, exceedingly in one place, (to artillery), impassable ravine, one piece was unfortunately lost .... The squadron of the 2nd Regiment of Dragoons under Major Woodford was early on the field, and much exposed to the enemy's fire, but the nature of the ground and the disposition of this line did not admit of those successful charges which their discipline and ardor, under more favorable circumstances, are calculated to make ....

The whole line was now re-formed on the borders of the woods from which the enemy had first been driven, when, night coming on and the storm returning, and conceiving that the object you had in view, which was to beat back the enemy that would retard our junction with the main body below [down river], to have been accomplished, the troops were directed to return to the ground near the flotilla, which movement was executed in good order and without any molestation from the enemy."

Battle of Chippawa, July 5, 1814

British: General Order, Montreal, July 13, 1814

"His Excellency the Governor-in-Chief and Commander of the Forces has received from Lieutenant-General Drummond the official report of Major-General Riall of the sortie which took place on the 5th inst. from the lines of Chippawa.

His Excellency laments the loss of so many valuable officers and men, but this sentiment is greatly aggravated by the disappointment and mortification he has experienced in learning that Fort Erie, entrusted to the charge of Major Buck, was surrendered on the evening of the third instant, by capitulation, without having made an adequate defence."

American: Major-General Brown to the Secretary of War, Chippawa Plains, July 6, 1814

"Sir, — Excuse my silence. I have been much engaged. Fort Erie did not, as I assured you it should not, detain me a single day. At 11 o'clock on the night of the 4th I arrived at this place with the reserve, General Scott having taken the position about noon with the van [vanguard]. My arrangements for turning and taking in near the enemy's position east of Chippawa was made, when Major-General Riall, suspecting our intention, and adhering to the rule that it is better to give than receive an attack, came from behind his works about five o'clock in the afternoon of the 5th in order of battle. We did not baulk him. Before six o'clock his line was broken and his forces defeated, leaving on the field four hundred killed and wounded. He was closely pressed, and would have been utterly ruined but for the proximity of his works, whither he fled for shelter. The wounded of the enemy and those of our own army must be attended. They will be removed to Buffalo. This, with very limited means of transport, will take a day or two, after which I shall advance, not doubting but that the gallant and accomplished troops I have will break down all opposition between me and Lake Ontario, when if met by the fleet, all is well — if not, under the favor of heaven, we shall behave in a way to avoid disgrace."

Battle of Lundy's Lane, July 25, 1814

British: District General Order, Headquarters, Falls of Niagara, July 26th, 1814

"Lieutenant-General Drummond offers his sincerest and warmest thanks to the troops and militia engaged yesterday, for their exemplary steadiness, gallantry and discipline in repulsing all the efforts of numerous and determined enemy to carry the position of Lundy's Lane near the Falls of Niagara."

American: Captain L. Austin, A.D.C. to Major-General Brown, to the Secretary of War, Headquarters, Buffalo, July 29, 1814

"They were met by us near the Falls of Niagara, where a most severe conflict ensued; the enemy disputed the ground with resolution, yet were driven from every position they attempted to hold. We stormed his batteries directly in front and took possession of all his artillery; notwithstanding his immense superiority both in numbers and position, he was completely defeated ...."

Attack on Fort Erie, August 15, 1814

British: General Lt.-General Drummond to Sir George Prevost, Camp before Fort Erie, August 16, 1814

"Dear Sir, — I have had a most painful and distressing duty to perform in reporting to Your Excellency the disastrous result of the attack which I directed to be made yesterday morning on the enemy's works and Fort Erie, an attack which there was no probability of a doubt but must have succeeded had the troops fulfilled that part alloted to them.

It signifies not to the public to whom the culpability of failure in military matters is attachable, the commander at all times falls under censure, however high his character may have been ....

An unfortunate explosion supposed by accident, of some expense ammunition in the demi-bastion of the works, by the destruction of many valuable officers and men, threw the remainder into such confusion and dismay that they likewise made a precipitate retreat, and the enemy remained in possession of his works."

American: General Gaines to the Secretary of War, Fort Erie, August 15, 1814

"Sir, — My heart is gladdened with gratitude to heaven and joy to my country, to have it in my power to inform you that the gallant army under my command has this morning beaten the enemy commanded by Lieutenant-General Drummond, after a severe conflict of near three hours, commencing at 2 o'clock this morning.

The Treaty of Ghent, December 24, 1814

The Mercantile Advisor, *New York, February 11, 1815*

"The great and joyful news of PEACE between the United States and Great Britain reached this city this evening by the British sloop of war, *Favorite*, the Hon. J.U. Mowatt, Esq., commander, in forty-two days from Plymouth."

Recommended Reading

The past few years have seen a treasure of excellent studies of the War of 1812 published. The following are recommended to provide the reader with detailed histories of some of the battles mentioned in the text:

Antal, Sandor. *A Wampum Denied: Proctor's War of 1812.* Ottawa, 1997.

Benn, Carl. *The Iroquois in the War of 1812.* Toronto, 1998.

Graves, Donald E. *Redcoats and Grey Jackets: The Battle of Chippawa, 1814.* Toronto, 1994.

———. *Where Right and Glory Lead: The Battle of Lundy's Lane, 1814.* Toronto, 1997.

———. *Field of Glory: The Battle of Crysler's Farm, 1813.* Toronto, 1999.

Hitsman, J. Mackay. *The Incredible War of 1812: A Military History.* Updated by D.E. Graves. Toronto, 1999.

Malcomson, Robert. *Lords of the Lake: the Naval War on Lake Ontario, 1812-1814.* Toronto, 1998.

———. *The Battle of Queenston Heights.* Niagara-on-the-Lake, 1994.

Turner, Wesley B. *The War that Both Sides Won.* Toronto, 1990.

———. *British Generals in the War of 1812.* Montreal and Kingston, 1999.

Associated Sites

Battlefield at Chippawa

Mailing address: P.O. Box 150, Niagara Pkwy., Niagara Falls, ON L2E 6T2
phone: 1-877-642-7275
email: npinfo@niagaraparks.com
www.niagaraparks.com
This battlefield, which sits on the Niagara Parkway south of Chippawa, has not changed significantly since the battle occurred in July, 1814. The Niagara Parks Commission has constructed a pathway and erected interpretive signs to guide visitors through the site.

Battlefield House Museum and Park

77 King St. West, Stoney Creek, ON L8G 5E5
phone: (905) 662-8458
email: bhmchin@binatech.on.ca
alpha.binatech.on.ca/~bhmchin
Built around 1796, this house sits on the site of the June, 1813 Battle of Stoney Creek. Dressed in period costume, museum staff demonstrate the lifestyle experienced by the family who lived in this house around the time of the war. The museum is surrounded by the 32 acre Battlefield Park, which is home to an impressive monument commemorating the battle. Another monument stands at Smith's Knoll.

Battle of Chateauguay National Historic Site

2371 Riviere Chateauguay Nord, PO Box 250, Howick, PQ J0S 1G0
phone: (450) 829-2003
email: parcscanada-que@pch.gc.ca
www.parcscanada.gc.ca/parks/quebec/chateauguay
The interpretation centre sits on the very site where the October, 1813 battle took place. Interpreters provide an introduction and lead a guided tour of the site's exhibit rooms. The centre provides an excellent view of the battlefield and is open Wednesday to Sunday, from May through October.

Crysler's Farm Memorial

Mailing address: RR #1, Morrisburg, ON K0C 1X0
phone: 1-800-437-2233
email: getaway@parks.on.ca
www.uppercanadavillage.com
www.cryslersfarm.com
This monument commemorates the bloody battle of November, 1813. Maintained by the St. Lawrence Parks Commission and the Friends of Crysler's Farm, the site is about 11 kilometres east of Morrisburg, Ontario. Atop a mound, a granite monument flanked by cannons overlooks the battlefield, much of which was flooded when the St. Lawrence Seaway was created in 1958. A mural, audio-visual presentation and artifacts await visitors to the Battlefield Memorial Building, at the base of the mound.

Dundurn Castle

610 York Boulevard, Hamilton, ON L9C 3J8
phone: (905) 546-2872
email: dcchin@interlynx.net
www.city.hamilton.on.ca
www.hpl.hamilton.on.ca/collections/landmark/dundurn.htm
This mansion was constructed in 1835 by Sir Allan MacNab, a veteran of the War of 1812. It sits at Burlington Heights, where the British and Canadian forces were headquartered after the fall of Fort George. The building has been restored as a museum and the grounds are now a park.

Fort Erie

350 Lakeshore Rd., Fort Erie, ON
phone: 1-877-642-7275
email: npinfo@niagaraparks.com
www.niagaraparks.com/historical/71-idx.html
Restored to its 1812 appearance and staffed by the Niagara Parks Commission, this fort is situated at the junction of Lakeshore Rd. and Niagara Blvd. Open mid-May to mid-September, the fort's interpreters help to create a realistic 1812 experience.

Fort George

Mailing address: P.O. Box 787, Niagara-on-the-Lake, ON L0S 1J0
phone: (905) 468-4257
email: ont_niagara@pch.gc.ca
www.parkscanada.pch.gc.ca/parks/ontario/fort_george
At the outset of the war, Fort George was a British military headquarters, and was Brock's centre of operations until his death. The fort was seized by the Americans in 1813, but recaptured by the British before the end of the war. It has been restored to its 1812 appearance and is maintained and staffed by Parks Canada.

Halifax Citadel

Mailing address: PO Box 9080, Station A, Halifax, NS, B3K 5M7
phone: (902) 426-5080
email: halifax_citadel@pch.gc.ca
parkscanada.pch.gc.ca/parks/nova_scotia/halifax_citadel
Although the present fort's construction was not begun until 1828, Halifax has been protected by a citadel since the mid-1700s. The third citadel guarded the harbour during the War of 1812. Today, the fourth citadel is maintained to depict the period 1869–71. It provides excellent views of the harbour and downtown, where the warehouses used by privateers during the war still stand.

Fort Henry

Mailing address: PO Box 213, Kingston, ON K7L 4V8
phone: 1-800-437-2233
email: getaway@parks.on.ca
www.forthenry.com
The fort presently on this site was completed in 1843 and is interpreted

to reflect the period around 1867. During the War of 1812, the fort was little more than a blockhouse guarding the entrance to Kingston, which was Britain's naval headquarters on the Great Lakes. The fort only saw action once during the war, providing cannon support during a battle between seven American ships and the British sloop *Royal George*. The fort is open from May until October.

Laura Secord Homestead

29 Queenston St., Queenston, ON
phone: 1-877-642-7275
email: npinfo@niagarparks.com
www.niagaraparks.com
Situated near Queenston Heights, this museum is the restored home of Laura Secord. Her dangerous trek through the woods to warn the British of an impending American attack is one of the great pieces of Canadian folklore.

Lundy's Lane Museum

5810 Ferry St., Niagara Falls, ON L2G 1S9
phone: (905) 358-5082
email: llmuseum@city.niagarafalls.on.ca
www.lundyslanemuseum.com
Although Lundy's Lane is now a multi-lane highway, the museum is situated on part of the 1814 battlefield. The museum preserves and displays artifacts from the battle, during which each side suffered about 800 casualties. Other exhibits cover early settlement and the Fenian Raids of 1866. The museum is open year-round.

Fort Malden

100 Laird Ave., Amherstburg, ON N9V 2Z2
phone: (519) 736-5416
email: ont_fort-malden@pch.gc.ca
http://parkscanada.pch.gc.ca/parks/ontario/fort_malden
Fort Malden was the British headquarters on the Detroit River during the War of 1812. After the war, the British built a new fort on this site (1838–40). Today, the site largely focuses on the fort's involvement in the rebellion of 1837 and 38, but its museum includes artifacts from the War of 1812. The fort is open from May 1 to October 31. Visitors should contact the site for visitation details during the winter.

Fort Niagara

Mailing address: PO Box 169, Youngstown, NY 14174
phone: (716) 745-7611
www.oldfortniagara.org
Fort Niagara, which houses the oldest building on the Great Lakes, is preserved as it appeared in the 1700s. Across the river from Queenston, this fort was taken by the British in December, 1813. To get to the fort from the Queenston/Lewiston Bridge, take the Robert Moses Parkway north. The fort is open year-round.

Fort Ontario (Oswego)

One East Fourth St., Oswego, NY 13126
phone: 315-343-4711
www.oswegony.org/history/fortontario
The fort is the fourth to sit on this site, and it has been restored to its 1867–72 appearance. The first was built in 1755, and the forts were successively destroyed — by the French in 1756, the Americans during the Revolutionary War, and by the British in May, 1814. Visitors to the fort can take a self-guided tour, and study a trove of artifacts housed in the enlisted men's barracks. The fort is open mid-May through October.

Queenston Heights Park and Brock's Monument

Mailing address: P.O. Box 150, Niagara Pkwy., Niagara Falls, ON L2E6T2
phone: 1-877-642-7275
email: npinfo@niagaraparks.com
www.niagaraparks.com
Sitting immediately on the Canadian side of the Queenston/Lewiston bridge, this park was the site of the Battle of Queenston Heights. In the centre of the park is a 50-metre tall monument to General Brock, which is maintained by Parks Canada. Visitors can climb the monument or take a battlefield walking tour. A monument to Laura Secord sits with a wonderful view of the Niagara River. The park is maintained by the Niagara Parks Commission.

Fort St. Joseph

Mailing address: Box 220, Richards Landing, ON P0R 1J0
phone (705) 246-2664
email: fortstjoseph_info@pch.gc.ca
parkscanada.pch.gc.ca/parks/ontario/fort_st_joseph
As soon as war was declared, the garrison from Fort St. Joseph was ordered to attack the Americans at Ft. Michilimackinac. Self-guided trails take visitors through the fort's remains, and exhibits at the Visitor Centre provide further information about life in the early nineteenth century. The fort is open from Victoria Day to Thanksgiving.

Fort Wellington

Mailing address: P.O. Box 479, Prescott, ON K0E 1T0
phone: 613-925-2896
email: ont_wellington@pch.gc.ca
parkscanada.pch.gc.ca/parks/ontario/fort_wellington
The first Fort Wellington was constructed during the War of 1812 to protect Prescott — an important link in Upper Canada's supply line. It was completed in 1814, about the same time the Treaty of Ghent was signed, and was abandoned in 1833. Construction to rebuild the fort commenced five years later. Today, the fort has been restored to reflect the year 1846. Parts of the original fort, such as the ramparts, still exist.

Windsor's Community Museum (Baby House)

254 Pitt St. West, Windsor, ON N9A 5L5
phone: (519) 253-1812
email: jcobban@city.windsor.on.ca
http://www.windsorpubliclibrary.com/hours/museum
This house, used by American General Hull as his headquarters following his invasion of Sandwich, is now home to Windsor's Community Museum. The museum is open Tuesday through Sunday year-round. Admission is free.

Fort York

100 Garrison Rd., Toronto, ON M5V 3K9
phone: (416) 392-6907
email: fortyork@city.toronto.on.ca
www.city.toronto.on.ca/culture/fort_york.htm
Although it is now tucked discreetly under the Gardiner Expressway on the west side of Toronto's downtown, this fort once dominated the waterfront. Fort York is home to Canada's largest collection of War of 1812 buildings and is open year-round.

Index